Richelieu

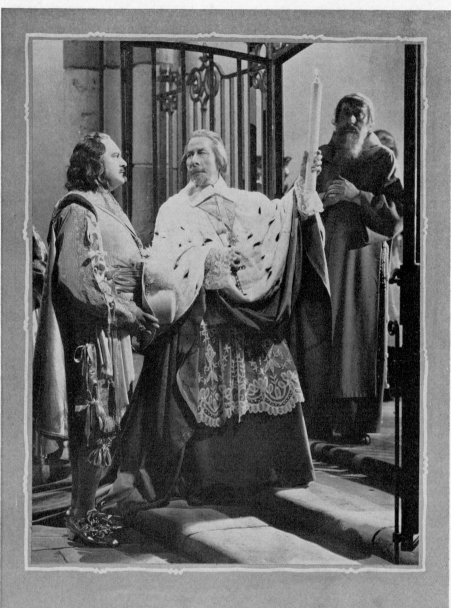

Richelieu

BY

RICHARD LODGE, M.A.

PROFESSOR OF HISTORY IN THE UNIVERSITY OF GLASGOW, FORMERLY
FELLOW AND TUTOR OF BRASENOSE COLLEGE, OXFORD

GROSSET & DUNLAP

PUBLISHERS   NEW YORK

Published by Arrangement with The MacMillan Company

CONTENTS

v

INTRODUCTION

THE history of France from the tenth to the close of the eighteenth century is bound up with the history of the French monarchy. Under the early Capets France was a mere geographical expression; its kings were little more than the titular chiefs among a number of feudal nobles, and their practical authority was limited to the Ile de France. From this powerless condition the monarchy was gradually raised by the energy of Louis VI., the prudence of Philip Augustus, and the legislative ability and high personal character of Louis IX. But the real founder of absolute monarchy in France was Philip IV., who created that administrative system which gradually extended itself over the whole kingdom, and undermined the independent local institutions of feudalism. Successful war and the extinction of the old mediæval families enabled the crown to bring most of the provinces under its direct rule. But a new danger arose from the practice of granting these provinces out as appanages to members

of the royal family, who formed a new nobility
as eager for independence as the feudal magnates
whose place they had taken. At the same time the
disasters of the wars with Edward III. and Henry
V. seriously weakened the monarchy, which sunk
again into impotence under John II. and Charles
VI. But the falling structure was successfully re-
built under Charles VII. and Louis XI. In the former reign the English were expelled, a standing
army established, and a revenue secured by the im-
position of the permanent *taille*. Louis XI. broke
up the formidable League of the Public Weal, and
the decline of the great Burgundian power on the
death of Charles the Bold freed the French crown
from its most dangerous rival. The marriage of the
heiress of Brittany to two successive kings extin-
guished the independence of the last of the feudal
provinces. The victory of the monarchy seemed to
be assured, when Francis I., at the head of a com-
pact and well-organised kingdom, successfully resisted the enormous but ill-compacted power of
Charles V.

But a subtle evil was already undermining the
foundations of this imposing edifice, and was destined in the end to overthrow it. This was financial

maladministration. The chronic deficit, which was the chief immediate cause of the Revolution of 1789, was already in existence in the sixteenth century. It is not a little curious that France, the home of financial theories, has only produced in its long history three great financial administrators—Jacques Cœur, Sully, and Colbert; and their efforts only succeeded in postponing the inevitable crash. Among the ruinous expedients to which the crown was impelled by an empty treasury, the most fatal was the sale of offices. This practice, which originated in the fifteenth century, was raised into a system by Louis XII., who is said to have copied the usages of the Roman court. In order to make these offices valuable their holders must be irremovable. Thus the crown, of its own accord, surrendered the control over its own officials. The administrative institutions, such as the parliament of Paris, which had been the most efficient agents in extending the royal power, became in the seventeenth century the most serious opponents of royalty.

The period following the death of Henry II. (1560) is the most critical in the history of France. A country on which geography had imposed the necessity of unity, and which had risen to greatness

in Europe by attaining that unity under a strong
monarchy, was suddenly divided by the most powerful of forces—religion. Not only was the practical authority of the crown almost annihilated during the long struggle between Catholics and Huguenots, but its theoretical foundations were torn
up and examined by polemical writers on both sides.
While the Huguenots endeavoured to conciliate
support by vindicating the independence of nobles
and municipalities, the Jesuits taught that the voice
of the people was the voice of God, and that circumstances might arise in which tyrannicide was
not only a right but a duty. At the same time military necessities forced the kings to intrust the government of the great provinces to powerful nobles,
who used their delegated authority in their own
interests, and threatened to revive a military feudalism which recalled the anarchy of the twelfth
and thirteenth centuries.

The struggle ended at last in the defeat of both
the extreme parties; and their defeat was due to
their collision with that passionate desire for unity
which has been the dominant force in French history from that day to this. The Huguenots, the
prototypes of the later Girondins, aimed at estab-

lishing a system of local isolation, which must have effaced France from among the great states of Europe. The success of the League would have subjected the Gallican Church to Rome, and would have made France a vassal and tool of the Spanish Hapsburgs. The victory of Henry IV. and the middle party, which represented national interests and instincts, was secured by Henry's acceptance of Roman Catholicism, and by his grant of the Edict of Nantes to the Huguenots.

Henry IV. is a great as well as an attractive figure in history, and he deserves much of the idolatry with which the French have always regarded him. He restored order after the chaos of the religious wars. He founded the Bourbon monarchy, which was to preside for the next two centuries over the history of France, and was to guide that country to an ascendency in Europe, to which it still looks back with boastful regret. With the aid of Sully he restored the balance between income and expenditure, and encouraged the development of the internal resources of France. He humbled the power of Philip II., and inaugurated the foreign policy which was followed with such success by Richelieu, Mazarin, and Louis XIV.

But the work of Henry IV. was still incomplete, when he was removed by the dagger of Ravaillac. Neither he nor Sully had the genius or the foresight to found a new system of government, which was necessary for the triumph of the new dynasty. Even in the task of destroying abuses, both king and minister were trammelled by their past lives, and by the circumstances under which Henry had come to the throne. In some matters a policy of compromise was all that was possible for them. Under their rule the forces of disorder were checked rather than annihilated. Again, the provincial governorships remained in the hands of the great nobles, though their authority was limited by the appointment of lieutenant-generals, who were to act as the agents of the crown, and by the policy of intrusting the chief towns in a province to persons independent of the governor. And the supplementary clauses of the Edict of Nantes conferred upon the Huguenots, not only religious toleration, but also a political independence which enabled them to stir up disorder whenever it suited their interests. Above all, the sale of offices, instead of being abolished, was systematised by the institution of the *paulette*. Members of the parliament and of the other central courts, by paying an annual tax to the crown, became the absolute proprietors of their offices, which they could transmit to their heirs or dispose of by sale to whom they pleased. Thus the office-holders in France came to form a vast hereditary corporation, with corporate interests to defend, and virtually independent of the crown. The nobles, the Huguenots, and the sovereign courts, were left by Henry IV. to be the great obstacles in the way of his successors.

The insecurity of the monarchy under these conditions was clearly manifested during the regency of Mary de Medici. There are few more depressing and wearisome periods of history than the first thirteen years of the reign of Louis XIII. The incessant intrigues of the great princes against the crown and against each other, the complete subordination of national to personal interests, the petty rivalries of the Huguenot leaders, Bouillon and Rohan, the coalitions against the queen's favourite, Concini, and against the king's favourite, Luynes, have been described in contemporary memoirs with a fullness which they only merit as an effective contrast to the state of things which preceded and which followed them. The regent and her ministers pur-

chased a few years' peace by lavish bribes to the
nobles at the expense of the monarchy, while she
sought to strengthen herself against domestic opposition by abandoning the foreign policy of her
husband, and concluding a close alliance with Spain.
The revival of the Hapsburg supremacy, threatened in the first period of the Thirty Years' War,
was allowed to progress without hindrance from
France.

From these disorders and dangers France was
saved by the greatest political genius she has ever
produced. No man was ever more completely a
politician than Richelieu, and no figure is more indispensable in a series which professes to form a
gallery of "Foreign Statesmen." His own memoirs
treat of nothing but politics. The character of the
man himself must be looked for in the accounts of
contemporaries, few of whom were able to estimate his greatness or to appreciate his aims. The
details of his private life have to be gleaned from
scattered sources, but chiefly from the letters and
papers which have been edited in so masterly a
manner by M. d'Avenel.

In writing the life of Richelieu one must narrate
the history of France and, to a great extent, of

Europe during an eventful period of nearly twenty years. Perhaps this consideration helps to explain why no first-rate biography of him has been produced, even in France. In spite of the innumerable books that have been written on this period, the work of Aubéry, although an avowed panegyric, and published as long ago as 1661, has never been completely superseded. It is to be hoped that M. Hanotaux may yet find sufficient leisure amid the distractions of political life to continue the great work which he has begun, and that this will fill what is an undoubted *lacuna* in historical literature. In the meantime this little volume can only attempt a brief estimate of the work which Richelieu achieved—and achieved with such success that he must be regarded as the chief founder, not only of France before the Revolution, but of much that is most characteristic of France at the present day.

CHAPTER I

RICHELIEU'S EARLY LIFE

1585–1614

THE family of du Plessis has no history. For generations it had lived in provincial obscurity on the borders of Poitou. In the fifteenth century François du Plessis, a younger member of the family, inherited the estate of Richelieu from his maternal uncle, Louis de Clérembault. His descendants were the du Plessis de Richelieu, and their chief residence was the castle of that name, situated on the Mable, near the frontier of Poitou and Touraine.

The first member of the family who played any notable part in history was François du Plessis, great-grandson of the inheritor of Richelieu. He rendered valuable services to Henry of Anjou during his brief tenure of the crown of Poland, and retained his favour when he returned to France as Henry III. Raised to the dignity of grand provost of France, François du Plessis became one of the most prominent and loyal servants of the last of the Valois. When his master died under the dagger of Jacques Clément, it was he who arrested the assassin and took down the depositions of the eye-witnesses.

The death of Henry III. left his Catholic followers in a difficult position. The traditions of his family seemed to impel François du Plessis to join the League. But he showed on this occasion a practical foresight worthy of his great son, and at once espoused the cause of Henry of Navarre. He had already gained the confidence of the new king by his bravery at Arques and at Ivry, and had just been appointed captain of the guard, when he was carried off by a fever during the siege of Paris on July 10, 1590.

François du Plessis was married to Suzanne de la Porte, daughter of the celebrated *avocat*, François de la Porte, and herself possessed of the practical ability which characterised her family. They had three sons and two daughters, and the youngest child, Armand Jean, was born at Paris in the rue du Boulay, on September 9, 1585. The child was so feeble and sickly that it was not thought safe to

have him baptized till May 5, 1586. His god-
parents were Marshal Biron, Marshal d'Aumont,
and his paternal grandmother, Françoise de la
Rochechouart.

Armand Jean was only five years old when his
father died, and his mother carried her children
from the capital to the seclusion of Richelieu.
There, amid the disturbances of the civil war between Henry IV. and the League, the boy's education was carried on for the next seven years. We
have no evidence that he showed any youthful pre-
cocity or gave any signs of future greatness.
Aubéry, who wrote under the auspices of Richelieu's relatives, and who would certainly have preserved any family traditions about his hero, tells
us nothing of this period of his life, so that we may
conclude that there was nothing to tell.

A distant province like Poitou offered few edu-
cational advantages in the sixteenth century, and at
the age of twelve Armand was sent to Paris, and
was admitted to the College of Navarre. There he
went through the ordinary courses of grammar
and philosophy, and an anecdote of his later years
proves that he retained a grateful recollection of
this period of his education. In 1597 Jean Yon, one

of the philosophical teachers of the College of Navarre, held for the third time the office of Rector of the University, and the young scholar, robed as a chorister, accompanied him on a solemn procession to the tomb of St. Denis. In later days, whenever the University wished to prefer a petition to the all-powerful cardinal, the venerable Yon was always included in the deputation. Richelieu confessed that he never saw his old teacher without a sentiment of respectful fear, and the deputation, even if its request were not granted, was certain of a gracious answer from the minister.

At this time Richelieu was destined for a military career, and he had only received the usual rudimentary education when he was transferred from the College of Navarre to the *Académie*, an institution founded by Antoine de Pluvinel to train the sons of noble families in the exercises and accomplishments which were to fit them for a soldier's life. It was here that Armand acquired the military tastes which never deserted him. He was at all times ready to exchange his cassock for a knight's armour, and equally willing to give his advice as to the handling of an army or the construction of a fortress.

The young marquis de Chillon, as he called himself at the Academy, was only seventeen years old when an event occurred which suddenly altered all his aspirations. In 1584 Henry III., in accordance with a practice not uncommon in those days, had granted to François du Plessis the disposal of the bishopric of Luçon. His widow, left in somewhat straitened circumstances, had found the revenues of the bishopric one of her chief resources. The episcopal functions were exercised in the meantime by one François Yver, who was avowedly only a "warming-pan" until one of the sons could take his place. But the chapter of the diocese resented the diversion of the episcopal revenue to secular and personal uses, and threatened to go to law with M. Yver, whose position was indefensible. In these circumstances Madame de Richelieu determined to procure the appointment of her second son, Alphonse Louis, to the bishopric. From 1595 he is occasionally spoken of as bishop of Luçon, though he never really held the office. Suddenly, about 1602, he absolutely refused to seek consecration, became a monk, and entered the Grande Chartreuse. In the next year M. Yver, on the suit of the chapter, was ordered by the parliament to devote a third of the revenue of the bishopric to the repairs of the cathedral and of the episcopal palace.

These events were a great blow to Madame de Richelieu, but she had still one expedient left. By a petition she delayed the enforcement of the decree of parliament, and in the meantime her third son was to assume the position which his brother refused. Armand seems to have made no opposition to his mother's will. In 1603 he quitted the Academy, and resumed his studies at the University. His eldest brother, Henri, was now at court, where Henry IV. had received him with favour as his father's son, and where he was able to defend the interests of his family. In 1606 the king wrote to the French envoy at Rome, urging him to obtain from the pope the appointment of Armand Jean du Plessis to the bishopric of Luçon, although he had not yet reached the canonical age.

Meanwhile Richelieu, who had taken deacon's orders and completed his theological course in this year, became impatient of the delays of the papal court, and hurried to Rome to look after his own interests. He succeeded in obtaining favour with the pope, and was consecrated by the cardinal de

Givry on April 17, 1607. There is no foundation whatever for the story told in later years by Richelieu's detractors that he deceived the pope as to his age by producing a false certificate of birth, and that when he afterwards confessed the fraud Paul V. declared that "that young man will be a great rogue." Equally unfounded is the counterbalancing story that the pope was so impressed with Richelieu's stores of theological learning that he exclaimed, *Æquum est ut qui supra ætatem sapis infra ætatem ordineris* (It is only fair that one whose knowledge is above his age should be ordained under age).

On his return he resumed his studies at the University until, on October 24, 1607, he was admitted a member of the Sorbonne or theological faculty. For the next year he remained in Paris, acquiring a certain reputation as a preacher, cultivating the acquaintance of all who might be of use to him, and retaining the favour of the king, who frequently spoke of him as "my bishop." From the first, his ambition was for political distinction; his avowed model was the cardinal du Perron, who had acquired a great but fleeting reputation as the champion of the orthodox creed against the Huguenots. Everything seemed to attract the young prelate to remain in Paris: in days when ecclesiastical duties sat lightly on church dignitaries, it appeared preposterous to expect him to reside in a petty, unattractive provincial town like Luçon, far removed from the capital, without society, with dull and depressing surroundings, and close to the chief stronghold of the heretics. Yet in 1608 Richelieu suddenly determined to bury himself for a time in what he himself termed "the most villainous, filthy, and disagreeable diocese in the world."

His motives for this step are wrapped in complete obscurity. It is certain that Henry IV., though no strict champion of discipline, approved of prelates residing in their sees. He may have hinted to the young bishop that his newly-acquired position carried some duties with it. But it is more probable that the decision was due to Richelieu himself. He was always keenly alive to practical considerations. He may well have felt that to obtain distinction he must do something to deserve it. His powers were immature, and he had no experience in the conduct of affairs. The bishopric of Luçon was not a great stage to appear on, but it offered opportunities for practical work, and its very neigh-

bourhood to La Rochelle made it the more important at a time when the position of the Huguenots
might at any moment become the most pressing
question of the day. It is possible that poverty may
have been another motive. The family estates were
fairly extensive, but they brought in a small
revenue, and Richelieu was the youngest child.
Even his elder brother, who enjoyed a considerable
pension from the king, was always complaining
of want of funds. Richelieu was throughout his life
extremely sensitive to public opinion. He could
make a respectable figure as a resident bishop on
an income which was lamentably meagre for an aspiring politician in Paris.

His first care was to provide himself with a residence. His palace was in ruins, and in those days
furnishing was a matter of great expense and difficulty. His letters to Madame de Bourges, who acted
as a sort of maternal adviser and purchaser for him
in Paris, are among the most interesting specimens
of his correspondence, and illustrate that careful attention to details which always characterised him.
The following was written in the spring of 1609,
when he had already been some months at Luçon.

"I shall not want for occupation here, I can assure you, for everything is so completely in ruins that it needs much exertion to restore them. I am extremely ill lodged, for I have no place where I can make a fire on account of the smoke. You can imagine that I don't desire bitter weather, but there is no remedy but patience. . . . There is no place to walk about in, no garden or alley of any sort, so that my house is my prison. I quit this subject to tell you that we have not found in the parcel a tunic and dalmatic of white taffety, which belonged to the ornaments of white damask which you have procured for me: this makes me think that they must have been forgotten. . . . I must tell you that I have bought the bed with velvet hangings from Madame de Marconnet, which I am having done up, so that it will be worth 500 francs. I am also getting several other pieces of furniture, but I shall want a tapestry. If it were possible to exchange the valance of silk and gold from the bed of the late bishop of Luçon for a Bergamasque canopy, like that which you have already bought me, it would suit me very well. There are still at Richelieu several portions of the said bed, such as the laths of the framework, etc., which I could send to you. You see that I write to you about my establishment, which is not yet well supplied: but time will do everything. I have secured a *maître d'hôtel* who serves me very well, and in a way that would please you: without him I was very badly off, but now I have nothing to do but to look after my accounts, for whatever visitors come to see me, he knows exactly what to do. He is the young la Brosse, who was formerly in the service of M. de Montpensier."

In another letter of slightly later date he shows a desire to impress his guests by his magnificence: "Please let me know what would be the cost of two dozen silver plates of the best size that are made. I should like to have them, if possible, for 10,000 crowns, for my funds are not large; but I know that for a matter of another hundred crowns you would not let me have anything paltry. I am a beggar, as you know, so that I cannot play the wealthy prelate; but still, if I only had silver plates, my nobility would be much enhanced."

But Richelieu was not only occupied with the splendour of his table and the hangings of his bed. That he was, by the standard of those days, an excellent bishop, there can be no doubt. In his diocese he first found an opportunity to display those

administrative talents which he was afterwards to
employ in the service of his country. His correspondence shows that he took the widest view of his
episcopal functions. Not content with admonish-
ing his clergy, and seeking energetic recruits from
all quarters, he also attended to the secular interests
of his flock. In the hope of obtaining relief for
their financial necessities, he writes urgent letters to
the assessors of taxes, and even to the great duke of
Sully. To his delight his merits begin to be appreciated. He hears that the cardinal du Perron speaks
of him as a model for other bishops to copy.

Of Richelieu's attitude towards religion it is not
easy to speak with precision. It was never the guiding force of his life; at all times he subordinated
religious interests to considerations of policy. No
doubt has ever been cast upon the sincerity of his
belief. Scepticism was in those days the luxury of
a few leisurely and self-indulgent critics. Richelieu's essentially practical mind was averse to the
speculative subtleties which lead to unbelief. Numerous passages in his memoirs show that he was
more inclined to accept the current superstitions
of his time than too curiously to inspect the evidence for them.

Still more difficult is it to lay down any formula about his relations with ecclesiastical parties. At the beginning of his career the chief divisions in France were the Ultramontanes, the Gallicans, and the Huguenots. To these were added before his death the Jansenists, a sort of advanced guard of Gallicanism. To the Huguenots Richelieu had no leaning, and he was ever ready to enter the lists of controversy against them; but he was always personally tolerant towards them, both as bishop and as minister. In a letter of 1611 he speaks of Chamier, one of their most vehement and outspoken champions, in terms of studied moderation: "He deserves to be esteemed as one of the most amiable of those who are imbued with these new errors, and if he may be blamed for anything besides his creed, it seems to be a certain too ardent zeal, which others might perhaps term indiscreet." With the sects of his own Church Richelieu's relations changed at different periods, and each had at times occasion to charge him with treachery or desertion. So far as their differences were doctrinal rather than political, he had no particular bias. He was a sufficient master of the scholastic theology for controversial purposes, as was proved by the works published during his lifetime. But the real object of these writings was to further his own advancement rather than to secure the acceptance of his particular views. He had none of the self-sacrificing enthusiasm and none of the deeply-rooted conviction of the religious prophet or martyr.

At one time there can be no doubt that he was powerfully impelled towards Gallican, if not Jansenist, opinions. One of the neighbours of whom he saw most was Chasteignier de la Rochepozay, the fighting bishop of Poitiers, whose father had been the friend and companion-in-arms of François du Plessis. The bishop of Poitiers had appointed as his grand-vicar, Duvergier de Hauranne, afterwards abbé of St. Cyran, and famous as the apostle of Jansenism in France. Another link in the chain was Sebastien Bouthillier, afterwards dean of Luçon, whose father had been the confidential clerk and had succeeded to the practice of François de la Porte, Richelieu's maternal grandfather. Sebastien with his three brothers formed a small bodyguard of devoted adherents to Richelieu, and at every crisis of his early career we find a Bouthillier at his side. The dean of Luçon was an intimate friend of St. Cyran, and it was he who introduced him to an-

other founder of the Jansenist sect, Arnauld
d'Andilly. These four young men, Richelieu, the
bishop of Poitiers, d'Hauranne, and Sebastien
Bouthillier, formed a small association for the pros-
ecution of theological study. Sometimes they met
together at Poitiers, but when this was impossible
they kept up a constant correspondence with each
other.

But intimate as his connection was with these
associates, Richelieu was careful not to commit
himself to their opinions. His published letters
prove that his aim at this time was to conciliate
friends on all sides, and to quarrel with no one who
could render him any service. He cultivated the
acquaintance of Bérulle, the founder of the
Oratoire, who established at Luçon the second house
which his association possessed in the kingdom. But
the most important friendship which he formed
during his residence at Luçon was with François
du Tremblay, already known as a stern monastic
reformer, and afterwards famous as Father Joseph,
"the gray cardinal." Du Tremblay, who belonged
to a noble family of Anjou, was eight years older
than Richelieu. Like him, he had been destined for
a military career, but at the age of twenty-two he

yielded to an irresistible religious impulse and dis-
gusted his family by becoming a Capuchin monk.
He became an active agent in the movement of
ecclesiastical reform which characterised the first
half of the seventeenth century. Among the institutions which were subject to his care was the
famous abbey of Fontevrault, near to which was
the priory of Les Roches, where Richelieu occasionally resided. In 1611 the abbess died, and Father
Joseph wrote to the court to secure the succession
of Antoinette d'Orleans, who had aided him in
introducing much-needed reforms into the abbey.
Richelieu received instructions to supervise the
election, and it was this affair which brought together the two men who were destined to be so
closely connected in the future.

Before this the death of Henry IV. had to some
extent modified Richelieu's plans of life. He realised that the regency of Mary de Medici inaugurated a new period in France, that retired
merit would be of no further use to him, and that
in some way or other he must thrust himself forward. He drew up a formal oath of fealty, in which
he and the chapter of Luçon expressed their devoted loyalty to the king and regent. This docu-

ment was sent up to his eldest brother to be presented to the queen-mother. But Henri de Richelieu, who was a great person at court, and one of the mystic "seventeen seigneurs" who aspired to set the fashions of the day, rather scoffed at this exuberant profession of fidelity, and suppressed the document, on the ground that no one else had done anything of the kind. This was not enough to discourage the aspiring bishop, who determined in the future to make frequent visits to Paris. He writes to Madame de Bourges to ask her to find a private lodging for him. A furnished room, he admits, would be more suitable to his purse; but he would be uncomfortable, and moreover he wishes to make a figure in the world. "Being, like you, of a somewhat boastful humour, I should like to be at my ease, and to appear still more so; and this I could do more easily if I had a lodging to myself. Poverty is a poor accompaniment for noble birth, but a good heart is the only remedy against fortune."

Richelieu spent six months in Paris in 1610, and though he did not obtain any employment, his time was not wholly wasted. At the house of the Bouthillier he made the acquaintance of Barbin,

who held an influential post in the queen's household. Barbin introduced him to Concini, and thus
established a connection with the favourite, which
enabled him five years later to enter upon a political life. But at this time Concini, though high in
his mistress's favour, had not aspired to influence
the government, which was entirely in the hands
of Villeroy, Sillery, and Jeannin, the veteran ministers of Henry IV.

Richelieu soon saw that his opportunity had not
yet come, and he again quitted Paris for his diocese.
But from this time he watched the development of
events with ever-increasing interest, and he had
made up his mind which side to take in the inevitable contest. The queen-mother had exhausted the
treasures which Sully had amassed in bribes to the
princes—she had given them offices, governorships,
all that they demanded. By these means, and by
dexterously playing off the Guises against the prince
of Condé, she endeavoured to maintain at least
the semblance of peace until the king should reach
his majority, at the age of thirteen. But her concessions failed to conciliate the nobles, whose requests became the more insatiable the more they

were granted. The ruling sentiment of Richelieu's career was his hatred of disunion and of princely independence. All his sympathies in the approaching struggle were with the court, with which he tried to draw closer the connection established in 1610. When the Huguenots in 1612 showed their discontent at the double marriage with Spain, and their leader, Rohan, made himself master of St. Jean d'Angely, Richelieu used his influence with the veteran Huguenot, du Plessis Mornay, to maintain order in his province, and wrote to the secretary of state, Pontchartrain, to assure him of his active co-operation.

His foresight had already perceived the means by which he was first to rise to power. He had no particular respect for Concini, who played a very vacillating part in the relations between the regent and the princes. But Concini's wife had that secure influence over Mary de Medici which comes from the habits of a lifetime, and the favourite might be a useful step in the ladder of promotion. At the beginning of 1614 the storm seemed at last about to burst. Condé and all the chief nobles, except the Guise party, had withdrawn from court

and were collecting forces. Concini himself, now
known as the marshal d'Ancre, who had intrigued
with Condé against the ministers, was in disgrace
at Amiens. Richelieu seized the opportunity to
write to him the following letter, dated February
12, 1614:—

"Always honouring those to whom I have once
promised service, I write you this letter to renew
my assurance, and to know if I can be of any use
to you; for I prefer to testify the truth of my affection on important occasions, rather than to
offer you the mere appearance of it when there is
no need: so I will use no more words on this subject. I will only beg you to believe that my promises will always be followed by fulfilment, and
that, as long as you do me the honour to love me,
I shall always serve you worthily."

On this occasion civil war was averted by negotiations, and the treaty of St. Menehould was signed
on May 15. Once more the queen granted all that
was asked of her. Every confederate received something for himself, either office, promotion, or
money. But among their demands was one which
was intended to express their devotion to the public welfare—the summons of the States-General.

This was also conceded, and the assembly was finally summoned to meet at Paris in October. The nobles had intended to use it as a means of advancing their own interests, but they were disappointed. The court succeeded in managing the elections, and the vast majority of delegates were devotedly royalist. Richelieu was active in the cause; and the exertions of his three friends, the bishop of Poitiers, Duvergier de Hauranne, and Sebastien Bouthillier, secured his own return as deputy for the clergy of the province of Poitou. As soon as the *cahier* of his order had been drawn up he carried it to Paris in October.

He was now on the threshold of his public career, and we may pause for a moment to consider the man himself, before attempting to follow him through the maze of intrigues in which he was so soon to be involved. His figure was tall and slight, but had not yet contracted the stoop in the shoulders which diminished his height in later years. His face was long and pale, with a prominent and well-formed nose, and surmounted by masses of long black hair. His lips were thin and tightly drawn, at times relaxing in a winning smile, but more often expressing stern resolution. Perhaps his most striking characteristic was a pair of bright penetrating eyes, under eyebrows which were naturally arched as if to express surprise. Clad in his purple bishop's robe, as he appeared at the meeting of the States, he was the model of an imposing ecclesiastic.

His great misfortune was his ill-health. During his residence in the low, marshy district of Luçon he had become liable to aguish fevers, which frequently reduced him to absolute impotence of thought and action. The energy with which he had thrown himself into his theological studies and the administrative work of his diocese had prematurely exhausted a frame which had been feeble from infancy. He was subject to excruciating headaches, which frequently lasted for days at a time. On one of these occasions he registered a vow, which has come down to us, and which shows the vein of superstition running through his imperious nature. If the Deity will cure his head within eight days, he promises to endow a chaplain with thirty livres a year to celebrate a mass every Sunday in the castle of Richelieu.

He was capable, as we have already seen, of inspiring warm feelings of friendship and devotion; but his own nature was cold and reserved. His letters of condolence, even when he writes to his sister on the death of one of her children, are as measured and formal as a diplomatic epistle. Few human beings, except his favourite niece, could boast a secure hold upon his affection. Throughout his life he held himself aloof from ties that might bind and impede him. Political interests severed him from many of the friends of his early manhood, as, for instance, from St. Cyran, and he had no hesitation in sacrificing them for the success of his designs. He could appreciate devotion, but he could not return it.

Richelieu set out for Paris in 1614 with a resolute determination to carve out a career for himself. In his bishopric he had learned to exercise his powers, and had acquired confidence in them. He was no longer troubled with the self-distrust which had led to his retirement in 1608. He had spared no trouble to form connections wherever opportunity offered, but he had been careful to avoid entangling pledges. That he had at all made up his mind to carry through the vast schemes of his later life it would be preposterous to suppose. His ability was practical rather than theoretical. His policy was always to make use of circumstances, rather than to attempt to wrest them to his wishes. His one firm intention was to raise himself to political power; and he had the sublime confidence of every truly great man that his own rule would be for the advantage of his country.

CHAPTER II

THE STATES-GENERAL—RICHELIEU'S FIRST MINISTRY

1614–1617

THE States-General, which met on October 27, 1614, are interesting as the last assembly held before the famous meeting of 1789. In itself, however, it was of very slight importance. The essential weakness of these assemblies lay in the deeply-rooted class divisions which ruined all prospect of constitutional government in France, in the want of any practical check upon the executive, such as is given in England by the control of supply and expenditure, and in the tradition that their only function was to formulate grievances. The great questions raised at this meeting were the *paulette* and the sale of offices, and the relations of the spiritual and temporal powers. The nobles and clergy agreed to demand the abolition of the *paulette*. The deputies of the third estate, most of whom belonged to the official class, were by no means eager for a change which would have deprived them of a valuable property. The instructions of their constituents, however, were too distinct for them to refuse their co-operation to the other estates, but they insisted upon complicating the question by demanding at the same time a diminution of the *taille* and a reduction of the lavish pensions granted by the crown. This last request was a direct attack upon the nobles, and a quarrel was imminent between the two estates, when attention was diverted to a new question.

The third estate demanded the recognition as a fundamental law that the king holds his crown from God alone, and that no power, whether spiritual or temporal, has the right to dispense subjects from their oath of allegiance. This at once raised all the thorny questions about the power of the papacy which had been discussed with such vehemence in France for the last sixty years. The clergy hastened to resent the introduction of such a subject by a body of laymen, and to point out that the acceptance of the resolution would produce a schism in the Church. The support of the court secured them a complete victory. Mary de Medici had committed herself entirely to an ultramontane policy which was involved in the alliance with Spain. She had, moreover, a personal interest in the matter. An attack upon the supremacy of the pope would cast a slur upon the legitimacy of her own marriage, which rested upon a papal dispensation, and consequently upon the right of her son to wear the crown. The king evoked the matter to his own consideration, and the proposition was ultimately erased from the *cahier* of the third estate.

Emboldened by this victory, the clergy proceeded to demand the acceptance in France of the decrees of the Council of Trent, reserving the liberties of the Gallican Church. The nobles, irritated by the attitude of the third estate on the subject of royal pensions, hastened to support them. But the obstinacy of the third estate, more royalist than the court, succeeded in preventing the carrying through of a measure which France had persistently avoided for sixty years.

At last the *cahiers* of the three orders were completed, and were presented to the king in a formal session on February 23, 1615. We have, unfortunately, no record of the part played by Richelieu in the preceding debates, but that it must have been

a distinguished one is proved by the fact that he
was chosen on this occasion as the orator of his
order. His harangue, which lasted more than an
hour, is said to have attracted great attention. That
it expressed his own personal views is improbable;
many of its sentiments are in opposition to the
whole tenor of his subsequent career. He seems to
have conceived that his duty or his interest compelled him to act as the mere mouthpiece of the
dominant majority, and to express opinions which
he knew would be favourably received by the
court. His whole argument is based upon the pre-
mises of ultramontanism. He condemns the practice of lay investiture, the attempt to levy taxes
upon the clergy, whose only contributions ought
to be their prayers, the interference with clerical
jurisdiction, and the non-recognition of the Council of Trent. Only two passages seem to express the
personal convictions of the orator—his vigorous
denunciation of the exclusion of ecclesiastics from
the control of affairs, and his lavish praises of the
government of the regent.

From this time Richelieu was a man of mark;
both Mary de Medici and Concini realised the
value of the services which he might render to

them, and his admission to political employment was assured. Henceforth his residence in Paris becomes more continuous, and his diocese occupies less and less of his attention. For a long time Concini had been kept in the background by the close union among the ministers of the late king, whom the regent had never ventured to dismiss. But this union had lately been weakened by a growing jealousy between Villeroy and the chancellor Sillery; and the chief link between them was broken in November 1613, by the death of Villeroy's granddaughter, who had married Sillery's son, de Puisieux. The discord among the ministers was Concini's opportunity, and he determined to make use of it to get rid first of one section and then of the other. His rise to power was accompanied by that of Richelieu.

In the autumn of 1615 it was decided that the court should travel to the Spanish frontier to complete the double marriage which had been formally agreed to three years before. Condé and the other malcontent princes had given their approval to the marriages, but they now refused to accompany the court, and set to work to raise troops in their respective provinces. Regardless of the danger,

Mary de Medici insisted upon continuing her journey to Bayonne. Her eldest daughter was sent to Spain to become the wife of the future Philip IV., and Louis XIII. was formally married to the infanta, Anne of Austria. Meanwhile Condé had collected an army, had evaded the royal troops under marshal Bois-Dauphin, and had crossed the Loire into Poitou. At Parthenay he was met by deputies of the extreme party of the Huguenots, who had already defied the royal authority, and the advice of their more moderate leaders, by transferring their assembly from Grenoble to Nîmes. They now concluded a close alliance with the oligarchical party, which pledged itself to prevent the recognition of the Council of Trent, to oppose the probable results of the Spanish alliance, and to maintain the Edict of Nantes. Thus the monarchy was once more face to face with the forces of disunion.

Neither Concini nor Richelieu had accompanied the court, and Mary de Medici was still surrounded by her old advisers. After some discussion in the council it was decided to adhere to the well-worn policy of negotiation and concession. The office of mediator was undertaken by the duke of Nevers and the English ambassador, and their exertions resulted in the treaty of Loudun, which was concluded in the spring of 1616. The treaty marks a complete momentary victory for the aristocratic party over the alliance between the crown and the clergy, which had signalised the close of the States-General. The king promised to give a favourable consideration to the demands of the third estate, to reject the decrees of the Council of Trent, to maintain the freedom of the Gallican Church, to respect the privileges of the parliaments and other sovereign courts, to uphold the existing alliance of France, many of which were opposed to Spanish interests, and finally to continue to the Huguenots all the concessions which had been granted to them by his predecessors. Secret articles stipulated for concessions to the individual princes, and the peace is said to have cost the king more than six million livres. Condé, who exchanged the government of Guienne for the more central province of Berri, was to be chief of the council, and was to sign all royal edicts.

The treaty of Loudun was followed by the fall of Sillery. As the chancellorship was, like so many other offices, a property for life, it was impossible

to deprive him of it. All that could be done was
to exile him from the court, and to intrust the
seals to a keeper, du Vair, who had acquired a reputation as president of the parliament of Provence.
But this first ministerial change was not enough to
satisfy Mary de Medici or Concini. Before long
Jeannin was deprived of the control of the finances,
which was entrusted to Barbin. Villeroy was not
absolutely dismissed, but he lost all influence. His
colleague in the secretaryship of state, de Puisieux,
shared the disgrace of his father, and his office was
now given to Mangot, an ally of Barbin. Concini
was prudent enough not to attempt to secure office
for himself, but the ministers were in the habit of
visiting him in his own apartments, and his vanity
led him to magnify the extent of his influence over
affairs.

The queen-mother had succeeded in freeing herself from the tutelage in which she had hitherto
been kept by the veteran ministers of her husband,
but her position was by no means secure nor satis-
factory. Since the majority of her son she had been
far more eager for power than she had been during
the regency. One of her most darling schemes, the
Spanish marriages, had been successfully completed.

But she was confronted by a powerful coalition of the chief princes, the third estate, and the Huguenots, and she had been forced to concede their demands at Loudun. When Condé came to Paris he was apparently all powerful. His palace was crowded, while the Louvre was deserted. Mary was naturally anxious to turn the tables upon her conquerors, and eagerly welcomed any assistance which promised to contribute to her success. These circumstances gave Richelieu the opportunity for which he was waiting. Whatever his personal opinions may have been, he appeared before the world as the devoted adherent of Mary de Medici and Concini, as the close friend and ally of Barbin and Mangot. He succeeded in obtaining the reward for which he was labouring. Early in 1616 he was appointed almoner to the young queen, Anne of Austria, and about the same time he was admitted a member of the council of State. He was employed on embassies to the prince of Condé and to the duke of Nevers. In August a royal edict granted to him an annual sum of 6000 livres "in consideration of the good and praiseworthy services which he has rendered, and which he continues to render every day." At this time it was intended to send him as ambassador to Spain to settle a dispute which had arisen in Italy with the duke of Savoy. But affairs at home soon became too critical for him to be spared, and the Spanish embassy was entrusted to somebody else.

The princes were unwilling to lose without a struggle the advantages which they had secured at Loudun. They were especially irritated by the influence of Concini, a Florentine adventurer who had crept into power by the favour of his wife. The court tried to separate them by stimulating their ill-feeling against Condé for having kept the lion's share of the spoil for himself. But hatred of the foreigner was stronger than their mutual jealousies, and in the autumn a general conspiracy was formed against the favourite. Its most active leader was the duke of Bouillon, the "demon of rebellions," as Richelieu calls him, and with him were combined Condé, the dukes of Mayenne, Guise, and Nevers. It was the first time that the Guises and Condé had been on the same side.

The coalition was extremely formidable, especially as its hostility could not be limited to Concini. The conspirators felt, though Condé alone ventured to express the general sentiment,

that the overthrow of the favourite would excite
the bitter enmity of the queen-mother, and that
they would never be safe from her vengeance unless
they could succeed in separating her from the king.
But Mary de Medici, thus personally threatened,
was surrounded by very different advisers to those
who had counselled the shameful surrenders of St.
Menehould and Loudun. It was resolved to paralyse
the opposition by a bold measure, nothing less than
the arrest of Condé and as many as possible of his
allies. The scheme was carefully prepared, and the
secret was wonderfully kept, considering the number of those to whom it was entrusted. Unfortunately, the queen-mother's irresolution allowed the
day to pass which had been originally fixed, when
most of the princes were at the Louvre. Meanwhile,
some suspicions were excited among the princes,
but Condé was so confident in his power that he
refused to entertain them. On September 1 he was
arrested as he was leaving the council, and was at
once imprisoned in a chamber of the Louvre.

The news struck consternation among the other
nobles, who hastened to secure their personal safety
by flight from Paris. As soon as they had recovered
from their first fright, they held a conference at

Soissons, where they agreed to raise troops in their respective provinces, to meet in twelve days at Noyon, and thence to advance upon Paris. Meanwhile, the prompt measures taken by the ministers had succeeded in preventing any serious outbreak in the capital, where Condé was extremely popular, and they set to work to sow dissension among their opponents. The Guises were soon detached from the coalition, and even the duke of Longueville was drawn over to the court by the influence of Mangot. Nevers and Bouillon, however, continued to hold out, and to prepare for civil war.

It is extremely probable, though there is no direct evidence, that Richelieu, as a member of the council, took part in the discussions which preceded the arrest of Condé. A vigorous policy was quite to his taste, and he had long been the intimate associate of Barbin, to whom, in his *Memoirs*, he attributes the chief part in these events. But one of the ministers, du Vair, was entirely out of sympathy with his colleagues. He had already proposed the release of Condé, and he now suggested calling in the parliament to settle the dissensions between the crown and the nobles. Such feebleness was intolerable. On November 25 the seals were taken from du Vair and given to Mangot. At the same time the secretaryship of state, held by the latter, was given to Richelieu, who, five days later, received a formal grant of precedence over the other secretaries. This completed the fall of Villeroy, who showed his resentment at being placed below his youthful colleague by ceasing to attend the council altogether.

Richelieu's first tenure of office only lasted for five months; but during that period he succeeded in imparting to the actions of the government a firmness and consistency such as had not been witnessed since the death of Henry IV. He had many difficulties to contend with. The departments with which he was especially concerned were those of war and foreign affairs, and both were left to him in the greatest disorder. The regiments were below their proper numbers, the commissariat was wholly neglected, and the habits of discipline seemed to have been lost. Money was wanting for the soldiers' pay, and on this, as on several later occasions, Richelieu found it necessary to make large advances from his own funds. As for the foreign office, the most recent and important documents were missing. He had actually to write to the existing ambassadors for copies of the instructions that had been given to them. But perhaps the greatest difficulty of all was interposed by Concini himself, to whose favour he owed his appointment. The favourite's head had been turned by his rapid rise to power, and it was doubtful whether his insolence or his incapacity were the more conspicuous. Richelieu has preserved the fragment of a letter to Barbin, which illustrates the way in which he treated the ministers whom he regarded as his tools. "By God, sir, I complain of you that your treatment of me is too bad; you negotiate for peace without consulting me; you have induced the queen to urge me to abandon the suit which I have commenced against M. de Montbazon to make him pay what he owes me. By all the devils, what do you and the queen expect me to do? Rage gnaws me to the very bones." France was weary of the caprices of a foreigner who had used his influence to amass riches and offices in his own hands. The ministers had reason to suspect that he was plotting to secure their dismissal, and Richelieu and Barbin actually offered their resignations to the queen-mother.

In spite of these obstacles, Richelieu and his

colleagues succeeded in dealing the princes more
severe blows than they had experienced at any previous period of the reign. Envoys were dispatched
to England, Holland, and Germany to remove any
suspicions that might have been excited by the
Spanish marriages, and to prevent any assistance
being given by these powers to the rebels. The instructions to Schomberg, the ambassador to Germany, were drawn up by Richelieu himself, and
contain the clearest exposition of the position and
policy of the court. At the same time three armies
were set on foot to act simultaneously in the Ile-de-
France, Champagne, and the Nivernais. Everywhere the royal troops carried all before them. The
eyes of Europe were fixed upon the siege of Soissons,
where the duke of Mayenne was blockaded by the
army under the count of Auvergne.

Suddenly the whole aspect of affairs was altered
by an incident which was entirely unforeseen.
Concini's unpopularity was a serious source of
weakness to the ministers; but the fatal blow was
struck from a quarter from which it was least
expected. Hitherto Louis XIII., who was only
fifteen years old, had been regarded as a mere cipher
in the administration. But the king had his favour-

ites as well as the queen-mother. Prominent among these was a young man of obscure origin, Luynes, whose chief recommendation was his skill in falconry. Mary de Medici and Concini had taken him under their patronage, and had thought to secure his allegiance by giving him the government of Amboise. But Luynes had ambitious designs of his own which were by no means satisfied by the position of personal favourite. He persuaded Louis that Concini purposely excluded him from affairs, that the princes were perfectly loyal and were only alienated by the omnipotence of the Florentine, and that the queen-mother was influenced by a blind preference for his younger brother Gaston. It was not difficult to persuade Louis to free himself from the galling yoke of his mother's omnipotence by striking a blow against a man whom he personally detested. The plot against Concini was arranged as secretly and successfully as that against Condé. No suspicions had been aroused in the mind of the favourite when on April 24 he was arrested on the bridge leading to the Louvre. He had only time to ejaculate, "I a prisoner!" when he was killed by three pistol bullets. His captors excused their precipitancy on the ground that he had offered resistance. All precautions had been taken. The queen-mother's guard was disarmed, and she found herself a prisoner in her own apartments. Concini's wife was arrested, brought to trial, and executed. The body of the murdered man was disinterred by the mob, hanged by the feet on the Pont Neuf, dragged in hideous triumph through the streets and finally burnt.

The news of Concini's death fell like a thunderbolt upon the ministers, who were expecting to hear every day of the fall of Soissons. Mangot was arrested, compelled to resign the seals, and then released as of small importance. Barbin, who was regarded as the chief agent in the late government, was strictly imprisoned. Richelieu alone was treated with some favour by the triumphant faction. He went boldly to the Louvre, where people who had courted him two hours before refused to recognise him. He found the young king raised upon a billiard table that he might be better seen by the crowd, and was assured both by him and by Luynes that they did not regard him as belonging to the faction of Concini. He was even granted admission to the council, where he found all the old ministers, Villeroy, Sillery, Jeannin, and du Vair in consultation. They received him with great coolness, and demanded in what capacity he appeared. On the answer that he came by special order of the king, they acquiesced in his presence, but he abstained from taking any part in the discussions, and soon afterwards retired. The change, however, was too complete and too sudden for him to retain his position, and he found himself compelled by necessity, if not by his own sense of gratitude, to follow the fortunes of the queen-mother.

CHAPTER III

RICHELIEU AND THE QUEEN-MOTHER

1617–1624

THE death of Concini and the fall of Mary de Medici seemed at first to effect a complete revolution. The rebellion of the nobles was at an end; in fact, they were received at court as if they had been fighting the king's battles against his enemies. But they soon discovered that the change of policy was not so complete as it appeared at first. They were jealously excluded from the royal council. Condé, on whose release they had confidently reckoned, was removed from the Bastille to Vincennes, but his prison doors were as securely guarded as ever. The nobles realised that the ascendency of the king's favourite was as intolerable as that of Concini. Nothing had happened to reconcile the hostile interests of the monarchy and the aristocracy.

The new government, though it had lost the opportunity of annihilating the power of the princes, was in other respects not wanting in energy and decision. Luynes, who took the chief conduct of affairs into his own hands, was a far abler man than Concini. He was determined to avoid the reproach of subservience to Spain which had been cast upon the rule of the queen-mother. French assistance was sent to the duke of Savoy, which compelled the Spaniards to withdraw their troops from Piedmont and to conclude the treaty of Pavia. But at the same time a resolute attitude was adopted towards the Huguenots. An anomalous state of things existed in Béarn, which was ruled by the French king without being united with France. Henry IV., after his conversion, had restored Roman Catholicism in his little Protestant kingdom; but he had left the church lands in the hands of the Huguenots, while the Catholic clergy received their stipends from the royal revenue. The French clergy had never ceased to demand that the Church of Béarn should be restored to its lawful possessions, and in June 1617 a royal edict was issued to gratify this demand. The Huguenots met at Orthez to protest, and the Parliament of Pau refused to register the edict. The struggle about its enforcement marks the beginning of the civil war, which ended in the loss by the Huguenots of their political independence.

Meanwhile Richelieu, with the permission of the king, had followed Mary de Medici into exile at Blois, where he was appointed president of her council. But he had many enemies at court, who persuaded the king that it was dangerous to allow him to remain in his mother's service. On June 15 he received a royal letter ordering him to reside within his diocese. He employed his compulsory solitude at the Priory of Coussay in composing a controversial work against the Huguenots. This took the form of an answer to four ministers of Charenton, who had replied to a hostile sermon preached before the king by Father Arnoux. The book itself is of slight merit, and its chief object was to keep the author prominently before men's eyes. It contains more vehement denunciations than arguments, and its intolerant tone is in marked contrast to Richelieu's own actions during his ministry.

The active defence of the orthodox creed did not suffice to secure Richelieu from the suspicions ex-

cited by his continued correspondence with the
queen-mother. Coussay was considered too near to
Blois, and early in 1618 he was exiled to Avignon,
where he resided for a year. He was followed
thither by his brother, Henri de Richelieu, and by
the husband of his elder sister, de Pont-Courlay. So
rigorous was the attitude of the court towards the
family that Henri de Richelieu was not even allowed to pay a short visit to his home on the death
of his wife. Richelieu, as before, solaced himself
with the labours of composition. His new book, the
Instruction du Chrétien, had a great vogue in his
own lifetime, when it passed through more than
thirty editions, but has since fallen into well-
deserved neglect. French prose was not then the
polished instrument that it became in the hands of
Pascal and Fénélon, and Richelieu, in spite of his
interest in literature, had little literary sense or
capacity. The only occasions on which he wrote
really well and pointedly were when his pen was
inspired by scornful indignation. A letter which
he sent about the end of 1610 to the grand vicars
of Luçon is in its way quite a model.

During Richelieu's absence from court the ill-
feeling against the administration of Luynes, in

spite of the success of his anti-Spanish policy in
Italy, was steadily increasing. He tried to conciliate
popular opinion by abolishing the *paulette*, but the
only result was to alienate the official classes, who
represented that he merely wanted to make money
by the sale of their offices. He showed no mercy
towards his opponents, and thought he could rule
by terror like an Italian prince. He did all he could
in the trial of Barbin to induce the judges to sentence him to death, and when a bare majority
refused to inflict a harsher penalty than exile, he
persuaded the king to reverse his prerogative of
mercy, and to commute the sentence to perpetual
imprisonment. The queen-mother was treated with
great severity at Blois; all her trusted servants were
removed, and their places filled by nominees of
Luynes, whose real functions were to act as spies
upon her actions. At the same time his personal
ambition was still more insatiable than that of Concini had been. He married the daughter of the duke
of Montbazon, afterwards famous as the duchess
of Chevreuse. He extorted from Mayenne the important government of the Ile-de-France, to which
he afterwards added that of Picardy. He was raised
to the rank of duke and peer.

The great nobles were furious at this rapid rise of a man, whose father, as they said, was the bastard son of a canon of Marseilles and his chambermaid. In their jealous indignation they rallied to the support of the queen-mother, to whom they had so long been opposed. The chief agent in the negotiations was Rucelai, another of the numerous Italian adventurers who had been attracted to France by the marriages of French kings with ladies of the house of Medici. It was arranged that the queen should be released from prison, and that the duke of Epernon, the veteran champion of the nobles, should undertake the task of aiding her. In the night of February 21, 1619, she escaped from a window of the castle of Blois by means of a rope-ladder, and succeeded in making her way to Loches, where she was received by Epernon.

The escape of the queen-mother caused great consternation at court, and preparations were at once made for the civil war which seemed inevitable. At the same time the struggle might be averted if she could only be separated from the aristocratic party, with which circumstances had forced her into an unnatural alliance. Richelieu's old allies, Father Joseph and Sebastien Bouthillier, suggested that he was the very man for the purpose. He already possessed the confidence of Mary de Medici, and his influence would serve to counteract the hot-headed counsels of Epernon and Rucelai. Luynes, who had never shown such hostility to Richelieu as others of his party, readily adopted the suggestion; and the sieur de Tremblay, Father Joseph's brother, was sent to carry the necessary instructions to Avignon. As Richelieu set out to obey the order he was captured by a body of soldiers at Vienne, but was at once released when it was known that he had instructions from the king. He found the queen-mother at Angoulême, where his arrival was resented by the councillors, who sought to monopolise influence over her. Richelieu's attitude during the next two years has often been a puzzle to historians, but it is really perfectly clear. The part which he had to play was a difficult one, and he has frequently been accused of betraying the queen-mother in the interests of the court. But the charge is absolutely unfounded. Devotion to Mary de Medici was rendered imperative by his interest, as well as by his duty, but he was under no such obligations to her associates. His clear and unmistakable object was to separate his mistress from the great nobles, and to effect her complete reconciliation with the king. He was conscious of a double allegiance, to the queen-mother and the king, and he displayed no common skill and dexterity in steering his course when the two points to be aimed at seemed to lie in opposite directions.

A personal quarrel between Epernon and Rucelai induced the former to urge Richelieu's admission to the council, which he had formerly opposed. His presence gave a great impulse to the negotiations with the court, and the treaty of Angoulême was hastily concluded on April 30. A complete amnesty was promised to the adherents of Mary de Medici, and she resigned the government of Normandy for that of Anjou, with the towns of Angers, Pont-de-Cé, and Chinon. Normandy was given to the duke of Longueville in exchange for Picardy, which Luynes took into his own hands. The partisans of Rucelai were bitterly dissatisfied with the treaty, which they had done all in their power to prevent, and their discontent had disastrous consequences for Richelieu. The queen had entrusted the government of Angers to his eldest brother, who received a challenge from the mar-

quis de Thémines, a member of Rucelai's faction.
In the duel which followed, Henri de Richelieu
was killed. This was a terrible blow to Richelieu,
who was sincerely attached to his brother. The latter was a general favourite at court, and, in the
judgment of Fontenay-Mareuil, he might, if he had
lived, have rendered valuable services to the great
cardinal.

The treaty of Angoulême was far from producing the results which Richelieu hoped. The dominant faction at the court remained bitterly hostile
to the queen-mother. When she met her son at
Tours, Luynes or one of his brothers was always
present at their interviews, and succeeded in averting the restoration of her influence. The king set
out to return to Paris, while Mary de Medici proceeded to Angers to take possession of her new
government. The desired reconciliation was as far
off as ever. The queen's adherents were treated
with marked neglect or resentment. A new guar-
dian, the Colonel d'Ornano, was appointed for her
younger son, without even asking her opinion. But
the most direct blow was the release of Condé and
the issue of a royal declaration in his favour, which
virtually condemned the queen and all who had

had a hand in his imprisonment. Richelieu in vain urged her to go to Paris, and to trust to the gradual revival of maternal authority over the king. She preferred to listen to the counsels of her more extreme followers, who wished her to remain at the head of the party of princes, and she demanded the dismissal of Luynes as an enemy of the state. It was the fear of this that had led to the release of Condé, in order that he might form a rival party among the nobles in opposition to the queen's adherents.

The year 1620 witnessed the outbreak of the civil war, which Richelieu had striven so desperately to avert. One after another the chief princes, Vendôme and his brother, Soissons, Longueville, Nemours, left the court with the avowed intention of resorting to armed force. Unfortunately all except Longueville hastened to join Mary de Medici at Angers, where they strengthened the violent opponents of Richelieu, while their jealous rivalry for the post of leader did much to weaken the cause which they had espoused. Their dissensions encouraged Luynes and Condé, now closely allied together, to take energetic measures. Carrying the king with them, they advanced into Normandy, where Rouen and the other chief towns surrendered in rapid succession, while Longueville fled to Dieppe without striking a blow. They then turned southward to confront the hostile coalition in Anjou. The most futile arrangements had been made by Vendôme and Marillac to resist the attack. Instead of strengthening the defences of Angers, which might have held out for months, they undertook to unite Angers and Pont-de-Cé by an entrenchment two leagues long, which they could not possibly complete in time, and which they had not men enough to defend, even if it had been completed. Richelieu pointed out the folly of the enterprise, but he was not in a position to insist upon his opinion, and it was probably rejected with scorn. The royal troops earned the position with an ease that was almost ridiculous. The rout of Pont-de-Cé became a byword in that generation. Vendôme himself was the first to carry the news to Mary de Medici, whose position was now hopeless. Richelieu urged her to cross the Loire and escape to Angoulême, where she could at least negotiate in security. But his advice was overruled by the cowardice of Vendôme and the countess of Soissons, and nothing remained but an unconditional surrender. Richelieu and the cardinal de Sourdis were entrusted with the negotiations on their behalf, and they were relieved to find that Luynes was ready to grant the same terms after the victory as he had offered before. The treaty of Pont-de-Cé contained no stipulations of any importance; it professed to be nothing more than a reconciliation, a mutual promise that all injuries should be forgotten.

Richelieu's attitude in these events is clearly expressed in his assertion that the queen-mother "was saved from ruin by her defeat." If she had won a victory, all the fruits would have remained in the hands of the princes who fought for her. As it was, she was freed from all obligations to them, and the way was opened for the recovery of her influence at court. His most immediate object was to effect a real reconciliation between Mary de Medici and Luynes, who was beginning to resent the pretensions of Condé, and was not unwilling to provide a rival to him in the person of the queen-mother. In the hope of effecting this purpose, Richelieu agreed to a marriage between his niece, Mademoiselle de Pont-Courlay, and the sieur de Combalet, nephew of Luynes. But the event disappointed his schemes, which were destined to be carried through in a wholly unforeseen manner.

The escape of Mary de Medici and the events which followed it had completely diverted attention from the edict about church property in Béarn, which had never been enforced. After the treaty of Pont-de-Cé, Luynes carried off Louis XIII. to suppress the resistance of the Huguenots. The campaign was soon over. Navarreins, the one fortress of the province, was compelled to surrender, and the Roman Catholic clergy were placed in possession of the ecclesiastical lands. A royal edict was issued to unite Béarn and Lower Navarre with the crown of France. Thus one of the great bulwarks of Protestantism was destroyed, the work of centralisation made a notable advance, and the king was received in triumph on his return to Paris.

Meanwhile the French Huguenots had watched the progress of events in Béarn with growing misgivings. The leaders of the extreme party determined to anticipate attack by organisation. In defiance of a royal prohibition, they held an assembly at La Rochelle and demanded the restoration in Béarn of the state of things existing in 1616, the

withdrawal of the garrisons recently established in
Guienne and Poitou, and the satisfaction of the
demands preferred in their last meeting. The king
offered to remove some of their grievances, but
ordered the immediate dissolution of their assembly. This was urged by Lesdiguières and other
moderate leaders; but they were powerless to control the more turbulent spirits, who believed that
the divided court would never venture on active
measures against them. In order to be prepared,
however, for every danger, they proceeded to
divide France into seven great provinces, in each
of which there was to be a military commander
and a provincial council. The supreme direction
was to be entrusted to a commander-in-chief, who
was to receive instructions from the general assembly at La Rochelle. As Bouillon refused the office
and Lesdiguières was suspected on account of his
relations with the court, the supreme command
was entrusted to the duke of Rohan, the governor
of St. Jean d'Angely. These preparations and the
evident intention to form "a republic within the
kingdom" excited the greatest indignation in Paris,
and Louis XIII. determined to crush the rebellion
by force.

Meanwhile Richelieu had failed to effect the desired reconciliation between Luynes and the queen-
mother, and the latter was jealously excluded from
the royal council. The marriage between Combalet
and Mademoiselle de Pont-Courlay had been completed, but it had failed to produce any confidence
between the two uncles. Luynes even took advantage of the marriage to endeavour to separate
Richelieu from Mary de Medici, by giving out that
the bishop of Luçon was now devoted to his interests, and that through him he was informed of all
the queen's secrets. There were not wanting advisers who urged Mary to renew her alliance with
the princes, and to try once more the chances of
war against the favourite. Richelieu, however, was
eager to prevent a coalition which he had been at
such pains to break up, and he succeeded in persuading the queen-mother to remain patient and
to avoid hostilities. This moderation enabled
Luynes to embark in the campaign of 1621. In
order to raise funds, he was obliged to restore the
paulette, and to raise a ruinous loan on the security
of the *gabelle* on salt. At the same time the office
of constable, which had been vacant since the death
of Montmorency in 1614, was revived and con-

ferred upon Luynes, although his military distinc-
tions were of the slightest. In May the king with
his army entered Poitou, and after a short siege
captured St. Jean d'Angely. After detaching
Epernon to blockade La Rochelle, Louis entered
Guienne, and for a time carried all before him.
These successes encouraged Luynes to undertake
the siege of Montauban, the chief Huguenot
stronghold in the south. But here his good fortune
deserted him, and after serious losses had been sus-
tained he was compelled to raise the siege. After
the death of du Vair, Luynes held the seals for a
short time, and this led Condé to remark that "he
was a good keeper of the seals in time of war, and
a good constable in time of peace." His omnipotence had been tolerated as long as he was successful, but his first failure led to the outbreak of
opposition. Puisieux intrigued against him in the
ministry, but he was still strong enough to maintain his position against attack. To recover his lost
prestige he laid siege to Monheur, a fortress near
Toulouse. There he was seized by a fever, which
carried him off in four days (December 14, 1621).
The reputation of Luynes has suffered from the
unpopularity which dogs the footsteps of fa-

vourites; but there can be no doubt that he deserves a more prominent place in history than has been usually allotted to him. He anticipated in some respects the future policy of Richelieu. He crushed a formidable coalition of the princes, and he inflicted the first serious blow upon the political independence of the Huguenots.

Richelieu and Mary de Medici had good reason to rejoice at the constable's death, but they soon found that all obstacles were not yet removed from their path. Condé and the ministers continued Luynes's policy of opposition to the queen-mother. Unable to prevent any longer her admission to the council, they did all they could to exclude her from any real control of affairs. The first subject of discussion in 1622 was the desirability of continuing the war against the Huguenots. Mary de Medici, expressing in council the opinions which Richelieu had drawn up for her, urged that civil war was rendered impolitic by the present condition of affairs in Europe, and that the primary duty of France was to check the growing power of the house of Hapsburg. But Condé, eager to separate the king from his mother, succeeded in persuading him to undertake a new campaign. The queen determined to follow him, but she fell ill at Nantes, and was compelled to retire to the waters of Pougues, whither Richelieu accompanied her. Meanwhile the king advanced into Poitou, where he defeated Soubise, Rohan's brother, and took Royan after a six days' siege. But for the second time he declined to attack La Rochelle, and leaving Soissons to cover the great stronghold of the enemy, he marched into Languedoc. In order to restrain the growing pretensions of Condé, the constableship was given to Lesdiguières, who was thus induced to throw himself altogether on the side of the crown, and to become a convert to Roman Catholicism. The chief event of the campaign was the siege of Montpellier, which was undertaken by Condé. But he was unsuccessful, and his failure enabled the moderate party to induce the king to agree to a peace. The treaty of Montpellier was arranged between Lesdiguières and Rohan. The Edict of Nantes was confirmed, but the Huguenots were only allowed to retain two fortified places, Montauban and La Rochelle. Condé was so indignant at the treaty, which was signed without his having any knowledge of it, that he left the court and set out on a journey to Italy.

This year witnessed an important event in the life of Richelieu—his elevation to the cardinalate. As early as 1619 Mary de Medici had persuaded Louis XIII., when she met him after the treaty of Angoulême, to demand this appointment from the pope. In the next year, after the affair at Pont-de-Cé, she induced him to write a second letter, and to send Sebastien Bouthillier to Rome to urge the matter on the pope's attention. For two years the faithful adherent of Richelieu remained at Rome trying to remove the difficulties in the way of the nomination. The chief of these difficulties arose from the resolute opposition of Luynes, and this ended with his death, but Richelieu always suspected the ministers of intriguing against his candidature. At last Gregory XV. was induced to grant the coveted dignity, and Richelieu received the news of his promotion in September. He went to Tarascon to thank the king in person, and Louis, who seems never to have regarded him with disfavour, told him that he could not have succeeded as long as Luynes lived.

Richelieu had welcomed the conclusion of the treaty of Montpellier as rendering possible a vigorous foreign policy in opposition to the threatening power of Austria and Spain. But he was grievously disappointed. The withdrawal of Condé left the chief power in the hands of Sillery and his son Puisieux, both experienced in the conduct of affairs, but inclined by temperament to half-hearted measures, and absorbed in the desire of maintaining their own authority. Even the queen-mother, so long devoted to the Spanish alliance, was at last awakened to the dangers which threatened France, and wished to abandon the vacillating policy which had so long been followed. This brought her into collison with the ministers, who sought to strengthen themselves by an alliance with the great nobles. When Condé returned from Italy they invited him to court in the hope of playing him off against Mary de Medici. But they were destined to fall before the opposition of one of their own supporters. They had obtained the removal of Schomberg from the control of finances, on an unfounded charge of malversation, and his office was given to the marquis of la Vieuville. But la Vieuville soon began to chafe at the subordinate position in which he was kept by his colleagues, and intrigued against them with the queen-mother. The discovery that considerable sums of money had passed through

the hands of Puisieux and had never been properly
accounted for, gave his enemies a handle against
him and his father. In January 1624 Sillery for the
second time was driven from court, and the office
of first minister passed into the hands of la Vieuville. But he soon realised that he possessed neither
the experience nor the capacity to deal with the
difficulties in which France was involved, and he
looked round for assistance. His connection with
Mary de Medici naturally suggested that he should
have recourse to the ablest of her servants, but
he feared that he would himself be overshadowed
by Richelieu's superiority. He proposed to form a
council for foreign affairs, with the cardinal as
president; but the members were to be excluded
from the council of the king. Such a position was
not likely to commend itself to Richelieu, and in
April 1624 la Vieuville was compelled to advise the
king to admit the cardinal to the council of state.
Thus Richelieu entered office for the second time,
and commenced an administration which was destined to be the most glorious in the history of
France.

CHAPTER IV

THE VALTELLINE AND LA ROCHELLE

1624–1628

RICHELIEU, according to his own account, pleaded ill-health as an excuse for declining the burdensome responsibilities of office, but his scruples were overcome by the urgent entreaties of the king and the queen-mother, and on April 29, 1624, he was formally admitted to the council. La Vieuville, who regarded his new colleague with the jealousy of conscious inferiority, wished to subordinate him to the chancellor and the constable, but Richelieu insisted on the right of a cardinal to precedence even over princes of the blood. M. d'Avenel has published an interesting document, in which the new minister drew up a comprehensive scheme of internal reforms. The decrees of the Council of Trent were to be accepted, but without prejudice to the rights of the crown and the liberties of the

Gallican Church. The monasteries were to be reformed and their number diminished, on the
ground that they were a serious obstruction to industry. The expenses of the royal household were
to be reduced by rigid economy. The *paulette* and
the sales of offices were to be abolished, and on the
death of existing office-holders the number of
places was to be diminished. To relieve the people,
the *gabelle* on salt was to be reformed so as to fall
upon foreigners rather than upon subjects, and
the exemptions from the *taille* were to be cut down
in number and refused in the future. Provincial
governments were only to be held for three years,
and all useless fortifications were to be demolished.

If Richelieu had carried out these reforms he
would have deserved the lasting gratitude of France.
But they represent the pious wishes of a newly-
appointed minister rather than the matured intentions of an experienced statesman. Possibly many
of the changes would have been repudiated by
Richelieu himself in later years; but at the moment
his attention was distracted from domestic affairs
by the overwhelming pressure of foreign politics.
Since the death of Henry IV. the policy of opposition to the house of Hapsburg had been abandoned,

with fatal results to France. In the great war which began in Germany in 1618 the emperor and the Catholic League had won a series of victories. Not only was the Bohemian revolt suppressed, but both the Upper and the Lower Palatinate had been conquered, and in 1623 they were transferred, with the electoral vote, to Maximilian of Bavaria. Ferdinand II., as the champion of the Counter-reformation, held a stronger position in Germany than any of his predecessors since Charles V., and he threatened to become stronger still, if once he could form an army of his own, and thus free himself from dependence upon the Catholic princes. Still more serious for France was the progress made by the neighbouring power of Spain, the close ally of the emperor. Philip IV. and Olivares were reviving the ambitious aims of Philip II. Their troops, under Spinola, had reduced the Lower Palatinate, and they now threatened to conquer the United Provinces, which could hardly make an effective resistance without support. England, which under Elizabeth had been a champion of Protestantism, and which had special reasons for sympathy with the Elector Palatine, was paralysed by the fatuous policy of James I., who allowed himself to be fooled by the prospect of marrying his son to the Spanish infanta. Unless resolute steps were taken, Spain threatened to shut France in altogether on her eastern frontier by a chain of dependent or subject territories. Negotiations had been opened with Vienna for the surrender of Tyrol and Elsass to the Spanish crown. And finally Spain attempted to evade the Alpine barrier which shut off her Italian territories from her possessions in Central Europe. In 1622 her troops had seized the important pass of the Valtelline, which connected Lombardy with Tyrol, in defiance of the claim of France to control the valley.

Sillery and Puisieux had fallen because they had failed to check the aggressions of Spain, and the task was now entrusted to la Vieuville and Richelieu; but they were hampered by serious difficulties in their way. France was a Roman Catholic country, and Richelieu was a cardinal of the Church. Though he might be willing to subordinate religious to political interests, and though he defended this by the example of the Roman court itself, yet he could not afford to give Spain the advantage of posing as the champion of the orthodox creed. Moreover, in France itself there was a strong Ultramontane party which resented any rupture with Spain, and Richelieu's patroness, Mary de Medici, would hardly pardon such a complete change of attitude as would appear to condemn her conduct during the regency. Above all, it was imperative not to entangle France in foreign relations which might advance the interests of the Huguenots. Thus alliances with Protestant powers could only be half-hearted, and accompanied with reservations fatal to their efficiency. Vigorous intervention in Germany, perhaps the best method of checkmating the schemes of Spain, was impossible, because it would alienate the Catholic League, which it was Richelieu's intention to conciliate, in the hope of playing the princes off against the emperor. The attempt to recover ascendency in the Valtelline was rendered difficult by the necessity of keeping on good terms with Rome, and of securing the Catholic inhabitants of the valley from oppression by their Protestant rulers.

Through these difficulties, which were not diminished by the absence of a good understanding with his principal colleague, Richelieu steered his way with a mixture of caution and resolution which does more credit to his intellect than to his con-

victions. France hastened to renew its alliance with
the Dutch, which had been broken off since Henry
IV.'s death, and to welcome the overtures made
by England. Buckingham's journey to Madrid had
resulted in breaking off the proposed Spanish marriage, and James I. now demanded the hand of
Louis XIII.'s sister, Henrietta Maria, for the Prince
of Wales. The negotiations were long and tedious.
Richelieu's claim to precedence as a cardinal being
disputed by the English envoys, he feigned illness,
and received them in his bed. But the great difficulty arose from the French demand that James
should promise toleration to the English Roman
Catholics, as he had offered to do in his negotiations
with Spain. The English king was willing to give
a verbal promise, but France insisted upon a formal and binding agreement, countersigned by an
English minister.

During the negotiations the differences between
Richelieu and la Vieuville became more and more
manifest. The latter assured the English envoys
that the demand for toleration was a mere form
to satisfy the pope and the French Catholics, and
that Louis XIII. really cared nothing about the
matter. The king, who considered that his honour

compelled him to exact at least as favourable terms
as had been proffered to Spain, was furious at this
attempt to frustrate his wishes. In August la Vieuville was dismissed, and Richelieu was left without
a rival in the ministry. His superior tact and determination enabled him to score a diplomatic
triumph. The English court, urged on by the reckless Buckingham, agreed to make the desired stipu-
lation, and to be satisfied with the barren concession that it should not form part of the marriage
contract. Father Bérulle was sent to Rome to procure the papal dispensation, and the marriage was
celebrated in the spring of 1625, soon after Charles
I. had succeeded to the throne on his father's
death.

If Richelieu, as he gives out in his *Memoirs*, was
the guiding spirit throughout this transaction, his
policy is open to serious criticism. Buckingham
wished France to assist Mansfeld in the recovery of
the Palatinate. Richelieu, on the other hand, was
determined not to entangle himself in Germany,
but wished to involve England in a war with Spain,
in order to divert Spanish attention from the Valtelline. His trump card in the negotiations was the
knowledge that Buckingham was resolved on the

French alliance, and that Buckingham dominated both James and Charles. This enabled him to make the alliance on his own terms. But it was extremely foolish, from the political point of view, to exact such concessions to the Roman Catholics. Not only were causes of quarrel certain to arise from so one-sided an agreement, but it necessarily involved the English court in a quarrel with the parliament, and without the supplies of parliament English intervention on the continent was sure to be futile. Possibly Richelieu may not have appreciated the importance of the parliamentary aspect of the matter, but it is more probable that he was not a free agent, and that the line which he took was forced upon him. It was not in his power to acquire all at once that ascendency over the king which he afterwards established, and in this question of the English marriage the real decision rested with Louis and his mother. If Richelieu had attempted to oppose them he would have shared the fate of la Vieuville.

France had been driven to renew her Protestant alliances in Europe, mainly by events in the Valtelline. This important valley, which runs from Lake Como into Tyrol, was the property of the

three Grison leagues, which themselves formed part
of the Swiss Confederation. Ever since the reign
of Louis XII. the Grisons had been the allies of
France, and had pledged themselves to close their
Alpine passes against the enemies of that country.
But for some time the Spanish governor of Milan
had been endeavouring by intrigues and threats to
secure the control of the Valtelline, and in 1603
the fort of Fuentes had been built at the entrance
of the pass. Since then a Spanish party had grown
up in the Grisons, and had set itself to oppose the
dominant influence of France. In 1620 this party
organised a revolt of the Roman Catholic population of the Valtelline against the oppressions of
the judges appointed by the Protestant leagues. The
Spaniards aided the rebels in expelling the Swiss
troops that were sent against them, and four forts
were constructed in the valley and garrisoned by
Spanish troops. The Grisons now appealed for
assistance to France, and a French envoy negotiated
the treaty of Madrid (April 25, 1621), by which
the forts were to be destroyed, and everything restored to its former condition. But the outbreak
of the Huguenot war encouraged the Spaniards to
evade the fulfilment of the treaty, and in 1622 the

Grisons, attacked simultaneously from Austria and from Milan, and despairing of French aid, made terms with Spain, by which they renounced their sovereignty over the Valtelline, and agreed to grant a passage to Spanish troops. The conclusion of the treaty of Montpellier at last enabled Louis XIII. to turn his attention to affairs in Italy, and in February 1623 he formed a league with Venice and Savoy to compel Spain to carry out the treaty of Madrid. The Spaniards, who were not prepared to embark in a new war, now agreed to submit the dispute to the arbitration of the pope, and the forts were handed over to papal troops under the command of the marquis of Bagny. But Urban VIII., although personally inclined to oppose the domination of Spain in Italy, was unable to resist the pressure of the Spanish party in Rome, which urged the impiety of restoring Protestant rule in the Valtelline. The terms which the pope proposed were so favourable to Spain that they were unhesitatingly rejected by Richelieu, who at last decided on energetic measures. In the winter of 1624 the marquis de Cœuvres, who had been sent on an embassy to the Swiss cantons, was ordered to raise troops for the reduction of the Valtelline. The attack was entirely successful; the papal garrisons were taken unprepared, and early in 1625 the valley and the forts were completely in the hands of the Swiss and the Grisons. At the same time, in order to divert the attention of Spain, the constable Lesdiguières was sent to co-operate with the duke of Savoy in an attack on Genoa.

But Spain could count on efficient supporters within France. No sooner had the government embarked in a foreign war than Huguenot discontent broke out into open rebellion. The Huguenots, who were still headed by Rohan and Soubise, complained that the treaty of Montpellier had not been carried out, and especially that the fortifications of Fort St. Louis, which threatened La Rochelle, had been strengthened instead of being destroyed. In January 1625 Soubise, who had already seized the island of Rhé, suddenly attacked and captured the royal vessels in the harbour of Blavet. This success was the signal for a general rising; La Rochelle espoused the cause of Soubise, and Rohan took up arms in Languedoc. The court was panic-stricken at the news, and a majority of the council wished to conclude a peace with Spain at any price. All Richelieu's firmness was needed to prevent an abject surrender of French interests in Italy. The great difficulty in the way of suppressing the Huguenots was the want of ships, and Richelieu resolved to obtain them from the Protestant powers. Both England and Holland were furious with the Huguenots for threatening to ruin the grand combination against Spain, and they promptly agreed, not only to supply vessels, but to allow France to man them with French captains and troops. Montmorency took command of the fleet and won a complete victory over the rebels, who were driven from Rhé and Oléron. Soubise fled to England, and the Huguenots hastened to sue for peace.

It was at this time that Christian IV. of Denmark undertook the championship of the Protestant cause in Germany. Richelieu considered that Spain, involved in hostilities with the English and Dutch, and pledged to the assistance of the emperor, could not act with energy in Italy, and that a very moderate effort would compel her to concede to the French demands. He therefore made use of English mediation to conduct negotiations with the Huguenots. This policy excited the bitter hostility of the Ultramontane party, who resented the collision with the papacy even more than the breach with Spain. This party was now headed by Bérulle, and it was supported within the council by Marillac, the controller of finance, and afterwards keeper of the seals. Virulent pamphlets were published against Richelieu, in one of which he was stigmatised as the "cardinal of la Rochelle." To conciliate his opponents, who might at any moment be strengthened by the adhesion of the queen-mother, he was compelled to authorise the comte du Fargis, the French ambassador at Madrid, to open negotiations with Olivares. But du Fargis allowed himself to be gained over by the Ultramontanes, and in January 1626, without authority, he signed a treaty with Spain. Richelieu, who saw clearly that powerful influences were at work in the matter, and who feared the alienation of Venice and Savoy, insisted on repudiating this treaty, and also another which du Fargis signed at Monzon on March 5. The final treaty, modified to suit the interests of France, was not signed till May 10 at Barcelona, but it is usually known in history as the treaty of Monzon. The sovereignty of the Valtelline was to be restored to the Grisons. Spain abandoned all claim to control the passes, and the forts were to be again handed over to the pope and destroyed.

Meanwhile the English ambassadors, ignorant of the events in Spain, were urging on the negotiations with the Huguenots, in order that France might be able to act with energy in Italy. Thanks to their exertions the Huguenots were induced to withdraw their demand for the destruction of Fort St. Louis, and to accept a very disadvantageous treaty on February 5. But, from the point of view of the government, the treaty had one very serious defect —that it was based upon English mediation. Charles I. had revenged himself for Louis's intervention on behalf of the Roman Catholics. The Huguenot deputies declared that they would never have accepted the treaty but for pressure from England, and for the assurance that henceforth "they might lawfully accept assistance from the English king."

For the moment, however, Richelieu seemed to have triumphed. He had humbled the Huguenots with the help of their natural allies, and he had forced Spain to resign her hold upon the Valtelline. But his very success had served to stimulate discontent at home. All the interests which dreaded the

growth of a strong monarchy combined against
the minister who threatened to destroy all restric-
tions upon royal absolutism. Even before peace
was concluded rumours began to circulate of approaching changes in the government. The personage upon whom all eyes were turned was the king's
younger brother, Gaston, whose succession to the
throne seemed almost inevitable, since Louis's
health was feeble and his marriage had proved for
many years unfruitful. But Gaston himself was
not very formidable; he was only the tool of those
who surrounded him. The real contrivers of the
plot were the marshal d'Ornano, whom Richelieu
himself had released from prison and restored to
his former office as governor to Monsieur, and the
duchess of Chevreuse, the widow of Luynes, who
had since married a member of the house of Guise.
It is difficult to ascertain their precise objects;
probably they had never distinctly formulated
them themselves. Their overt measures were to demand the admission of Gaston to the council, and
to oppose the plan of marrying him to Mademoiselle de Montpensier. Rumour accused them of having further designs: to remove Louis XIII. to a
monastery, to place Gaston on the throne, and to

marry him to Anne of Austria. The latter is said
to have exclaimed in answer to the charge, "I should
not have gained enough by the change." It is certain, at all events, that the conspiracy was directed
against Richelieu, whose removal was a necessary
preliminary to any further measures. Nearly all
the princes were more or less involved: Condé because he resented his continued exclusion from the
court; the young Soissons, because he wished to
secure the Montpensier inheritance for himself;
the rest from a general desire to increase their
own importance and independence. To the Frenchmen of the seventeenth century a plot was an at-
traction itself; they did not need any carefully-
prepared schemes or skilfully-dangled bribes to
induce them to embark in it. According to Richelieu, foreign powers were also implicated. England,
Holland, and Savoy all resented the conclusion of
the treaty of Monzon, and were willing to overthrow the statesman whom they considered responsible; while Spain was always on the look-out
for the opportunity of stirring up domestic disorder in France.

The plotters seemed to have talked with a reckless indiscretion, which had been natural enough

under the feeble regency, but which was madness now that power had fallen to a man capable and willing to use it. Richelieu waited till he had collected enough evidence to satisfy the king, and then struck with vigour and decision.

On May 4, Ornano was seized and imprisoned at Vincennes, where he died four months later. Gaston went in a rage to the cardinal, who firmly accepted the responsibility for the action. To most of the conspirators little severity was shown. The king's half-brothers, the duke of Vendôme and the Grand Prior, were taken prisoners, and Madame de Chevreuse, exiled from the court, escaped to Lorraine. Condé hastened to come to terms with the government, and the other princes were treated with passive contempt. Gaston, who was formally reconciled with Louis and his mother, received the duchies of Orleans and Chartres as an appanage, and Richelieu himself officiated at his marriage with Mademoiselle de Montpensier. But while a politic clemency spared the leaders, one of their tools was selected for condign punishment, as an example of the dangers of conspiring. Henri de Talleyrand, count of Chalais, whose mother had bought for him the office of master of the wardrobe, had been drawn into the plot by the seductive charms of the duchess of Chevreuse. His youthful indiscretion had led him into foolish conversations, which were now brought up against him. He was tried before a specially appointed commission, and was condemned to be beheaded and quartered. In spite of the frantic supplications of his mother, the sentence was carried out. That he was more or less guilty there is little doubt; but he was far less to blame than others who escaped, and his untimely fate will always excite a feeling of indignation against the ruthless policy which chose him as a sacrifice.

The inevitable result of this abortive conspiracy was to strengthen the minister against whom it was directed. The king granted Richelieu a body-guard of a hundred men, to protect him against the malice of his enemies. His control over the government became the more absolute as it appeared that he was the necessary bulwark of the royal power. At this moment the constableship was left vacant by the death of the veteran Lesdiguières, and Richelieu seized the opportunity to suppress an office which gave excessive authority and independence to its holder. The corresponding office of admiral was purchased from Montmorency for 1,200,000 livres, and was also suppressed. Thus the army and navy were brought under the direct control of the ministers, and a great step was taken in the process of centralisation. Richelieu himself was profoundly impressed with the necessity of making France a great naval power, in order to protect and extend French commerce, and to avoid the humiliation of depending for foreign assistance against Huguenot rebellion. To give him the necessary authority, the king conferred upon him the novel office of "grand-master, chief, and superintendent-general of navigation and commerce." Large sums of money were raised to build and purchase ships, and to furnish them with crews and necessary stores. As a navy in those days must be based upon a large mercantile marine, Richelieu projected the formation of a great company at Morbihan, which should dispute the trade with the East and West Indies, with England, Holland, and Spain.

Richelieu's measures were not only dictated by a wise comprehension of the future interests of France: his gaze was never long withdrawn from the immediate drama of foreign affairs. The Protestant cause in Europe, with which France could not but be intimately connected, had suffered severe blows in 1626. Christian IV. of Denmark had been crushed by Tilly and the troops of the Catholic League; Mansfeld had been irretrievably defeated by the imperial army under Wallenstein. To make matters worse, England, which was more responsible than any other power for the failure of the Danish king, and which had failed in its own naval attack upon Spain, did not hesitate to add to its difficulties by picking a quarrel with France. The marriage contract of Henrietta Maria had produced nothing but quarrels and misunderstandings between the two powers. Charles I. could not grant the promised toleration to the Roman Catholics in face of parliamentary opposition, and so he calmly repudiated his promise and allowed the penal laws to be enforced. He quarrelled with his wife for her avowed partiality for her native country and her own religion. So far did his anger carry him that he expelled with insult the French ladies and priests of the queen's household. He resented the maritime schemes of Richelieu as an encroachment upon the naval supremacy which he claimed as England's right. English cruisers captured French vessels on the slightest pretext, and their cargoes were sold by order of the English courts as contraband of war.

So far as these disputes constituted causes of war, it was France which had most cause of complaint. But indignant as Louis XIII. and Mary de Medici might be at the treatment of Henrietta Maria and the shameless disregard of the marriage contract, they would have been restrained by Richelieu from endeavouring to redress their grievances by arms. It was England which embarked upon the war, and her conduct was so obviously fatuous under existing circumstances that men were at a loss to account for it. The real author of the French war, as of the French alliance, was Buckingham. When he had visited France to escort Charles I.'s bride to England, he had been audacious enough to make open love to Anne of Austria, the neglected wife of Louis XIII. Since then he had several times suggested his return to Paris as envoy for the settlement of disputes, but his proposal had always been rejected by the king and queen-mother, who had no desire that he should carry his insolent overtures any further. Contemporaries did not hesitate to assert and to believe that the proud favourite considered himself insulted, and that he revenged him-

self by attacking France. It is more probable that
he wished to conciliate the hostile majority in parliament, who had never forgiven him for allow-
ing English ships to be employed against the
Huguenots. With a sublime self-confidence which
no failure had been able to weaken, he believed
that his enterprise would be irresistible, and that
a rapid success would give him a position in England which nothing could shake. Although the
Huguenots were not in revolt, he announced himself as the champion of their interests, and complained that the recent treaty had been broken by
the retention of Fort St. Louis, and by the construction of the two forts of St. Martin and La
Prée on the island of Rhé, which commanded the
entrance to the harbour of La Rochelle. No pains
were spared in fitting out the fleet, which sailed
from Stokes Bay on June 27, 1627. Its exact des-
tination was at first uncertain, but on July 10 it
anchored off the coast of Rhé. Two days later the
troops were landed after a stubborn struggle, and
proceeded to lay siege to the fort of St. Martin.

It was a critical moment in the career of Richelieu. Louis XIII. was ill with a tertian fever, and
the cardinal did not dare to leave him. Yet upon

him fell all the responsibility of resisting an invasion, which had been foreseen but very insufficiently provided against. And the English were not the only enemies to be considered. Rohan, urged on by Buckingham, hastened to raise once more the standard of revolt in Languedoc. La Rochelle was at first inclined to resent an enterprise about which it had never been consulted, and to remain obstinately neutral. But it was certain that the citizens would be forced before long to espouse the English cause. And Buckingham had made careful preparations to divert the attention of France. His envoy had gained over Charles IV. at Lorraine, at whose court the duchess of Chevreuse continued her incessant intrigues against Richelieu. The discontented court of Soissons was at Turin, and both Savoy and Venice only waited for the news of an English victory to join the coalition against France. And within France itself there were many opponents of the cardinal who would have welcomed a defeat which should discredit his administration. He had no ally to look to except Spain, with whom France had concluded a treaty in April. But it was notorious that Spain only desired to embroil France with England, and that Olivares had ac-

tually revealed the treaty to Buckingham in order
to induce him to accept his terms. The most immediate danger, however, was in the island of
Rhé. Toiras, the commander, had received lavish
grants of money, but had neglected to hurry on
his preparations. Neither of the two forts was in
a condition to resist attack, and at the moment of
his landing Buckingham might have carried either
of them by assault. But he paid no attention to La
Prée, and wasted four days before reaching St.
Martin. His delay enabled the garrison by great
exertion to complete the defences just in time, and
the English were compelled to abandon the assault
for a blockade. This gave the French time to or-
ganize the relief of the fortress; but the matter
was still urgent. Toiras had barely food enough to
last two months, and his needs were increased when
Buckingham collected the mothers, wives, and
daughters of the garrison, and drove them into the
fortress by a volley of English bullets. As the English naval force was superior to any that France
could bring against it, and as the assailants must
sooner or later have the co-operation of La Rochelle, it seemed as if the surrender of the fort was
only a question of time.

But Richelieu's energy rose to the occasion. Though he spent the whole day and many nights by the king's bed, and was compelled to disguise his anxieties for fear of alarming the patient, he undertook the whole superintendence of the necessary measures for the relief of St. Martin. He had the capacity, which seems peculiar to great statesmen, of grasping every minute detail as clearly as the general outline of a scheme. Nothing was too small for him, and he shrank from no labour or responsibility. The duke of Angoulême was appointed to command the army in Poitou, with instructions to watch over La Rochelle and prevent any assistance being given to the English. Before long it was found necessary to extend this supervision to a regular siege. Agents were sent in every direction to collect sailors, ships, and provisions, at the ports of Brouage and the Sables d'Olonne. Special care was taken to provide a number of pinnaces and rowing-boats from Bayonne, so that the relieving force might be independent of the wind, and might evade the shallows of a low tide. Succour was sent to the island of Oléron, which was more fertile than Rhé, and which would become of immense importance if the latter were lost. The Span-

ish offers of assistance were accepted, though
Richelieu had little confidence in their good faith,
and the subsidy treaty was renewed with the
Dutch, so as to secure at least their neutrality. As
the treasury was wholly unable to meet the extraordinary expenditure, Richelieu employed his own
money and his own credit to supply the deficiency.

Before the end of August the king was well
enough to travel, and he and Richelieu at once set
out to join the army before La Rochelle. Their arrival did much to stimulate the exertions to assist
the besieged fort, but though some few supplies
had been smuggled in, nothing substantial had been
achieved. The garrison was more and more pressed
by want, and on September 25 an offer of surrender was actually made, but postponed to the
next day. That very evening the wind took a favourable turn, and the relieving force succeeded in
making its way through the English fleet, with the
loss of only one boat. St. Martin was safe for
nearly six weeks. For the moment the English were
so discouraged as to decide on abandoning the enterprise, but the promise of speedy reinforcements
induced them to change their mind. But the English administration was hopelessly corrupt and in-

efficient, and Charles's good-will was not enough
to fit out the ships in time, or to provide favourable winds when they were ready. Meanwhile the
besiegers were suffering from the inclemency of
an early winter, and found themselves in danger of
being in their turn besieged. Richelieu had succeeded in sending troops across to the island, where
they found a safe shelter in the neglected fort of
La Prée. It was known that Toiras could not hold
out beyond November 5, but Buckingham could
not hold out so long. On October 27 he made a
futile attempt to storm the fort, and two days
later he proceeded to embark his troops. But Marshal Schomberg brought up the newly-arrived
soldiers from La Prée, and the English retreat was
turned into a confused and ruinous rout. Buckingham returned to England with barely a third of
the force that had accompanied him. Some three
weeks later the Spanish fleet, which a little before
might have rendered invaluable services, arrived
at Morbihan.

The English invasion had forced Richelieu into
a closer alliance with the ultra-Catholic party than
he would have formed of his own accord, and he
found it advisable to cement the alliance by induc-

ing the pope to give the cardinal's hat to Bérulle, though the latter was his avowed rival for the favour of the queen-mother. The full extent of the dangers which threatened France had been recently revealed by the papers of Montague, the English envoy, who had been captured on the borders of Lorraine. These disclosed, not only the intrigues of Buckingham with Lorraine, Savoy and the count of Soissons, but also a design on the part of the emperor to assert his claim to the bishoprics of Metz, Toul, and Verdun, which had been occupied by France since 1553, but had never been resigned by the Empire. Some documents found in Buckingham's camp at St. Martin also revealed the intrigues of Spain with England. But Richelieu determined to disregard as much as possible these external dangers, and to concentrate his attention upon the siege of La Rochelle. The task of making head against Rohan in Languedoc was entrusted to Condé, a notorious hater of the religion which his fathers had professed, and to Montmorency, the governor of the province. The king and cardinal set to work to form an efficient blockade of the Huguenot stronghold in the west. The three commanders of the army, Angoulême, Schomberg, and

Bassompierre, undertook to close all access to the
town by land by the construction of a line of
fortifications, three leagues in length, which were
defended by eleven forts and eighteen redoubts. But
relief from the land side was little to be dreaded,
and the most serious problem was to close the entrance to the harbour. This was the special care of
Richelieu himself. Acting on the advice of two
French engineers, he ordered the construction of
two great moles, one from each side of the harbour,
at a sufficient distance from the town to be out of
range of cannon-shot. The moles were to be built
of huge stones, with a slope on each side, so as to
break the force of the waves. In the middle a space
was to be left for the tide to go in and out, but
this was to be partially blocked by sunken ships,
and to be guarded by the French fleet. In January
this fleet arrived from Morbihan under the command of the duke of Guise, and with it came the
Spanish vessels which had professed to come for
the relief of St. Martin. But they had scarcely
been eight days at anchor when a false report of
the approach of the English compelled the Spaniards to show their true colours, and to demand
leave to depart. The officers themselves were

ashamed of the part which they had to play, and which they vainly tried to excuse on the ground of necessary preparation for a joint attack upon England in the summer.

Richelieu had other difficulties to contend with besides the fury of the winds, the heroic obstinacy of the besieged citizens, and the aid which was promised to them by England. All whose interests were opposed to the strengthening of the monarchy looked forward to the fall of La Rochelle with serious misgivings. Bassompierre only expressed the prevalent sentiment of his class when he exclaimed, "We shall be fools enough to take the city." The most careful supervision and the exercise of sovereign authority were needed to prevent careless or treasonable neglect of the siege operations. It was, therefore, a heavy blow to him when he learnt that Louis XIII., weary of the monotony of camp life, and dreading the winter climate on the salt marshes, announced his determination to return to Paris. At first he risked the royal displeasure by opposing the king's wishes, and when he had to give way, he found it necessary to offer an opportunity for the intrigues of his opponents by consenting to remain at La Rochelle. Fortunately Louis was capable of appreciating his devotion. Not only did he entrust Richelieu during his absence with the supreme command by sea and land, but he resisted the attempts of his mother to prolong his stay in the capital, and in April had once more returned to the siege.

Richelieu had now the opportunity of displaying the military tastes and capacity which he had developed in his younger days. Attired in a garb which betrayed the soldier rather than the ecclesiastic, he undertook the personal direction of the siege works by land and sea. The strictest discipline was maintained, and the cardinal triumphantly compared his camp to a well-ordered monastery. The men were well paid, well fed, and well clothed—a striking contrast to the condition of most of the armies of that period,—and the amount of sickness was surprisingly small. Steady progress was made with the moles, though the ravages of the sea more than once made it necessary to do much of the work over again; but each time some lesson was learnt and some fault of construction was remedied. Richelieu had good reason for energetic action, when he heard that the queen-mother had joined the ranks of his opponents, and that war

had broken out in Italy about the succession to
Mantua and Montferrat. Twice he tried to surprise
the town during the night, but both attempts
failed, and he had to trust to the slow but certain
results of the blockade. The return of the king removed some of his worst anxieties, but he was still
worried by the urgent necessity of relieving Casale,
which was besieged by the Spaniards. He could,
however, do nothing till La Rochelle had fallen.
In May an English fleet under Lord Denbigh sailed
to relieve the town, but it was ill-equipped, and the
sailors were the discontented victims of impress-
ment. After viewing the defences of the harbour,
and upbraiding the deputies from La Rochelle for
their false information, the English retired without
striking a blow, but promising that they would
return with a stronger force. Meanwhile the besieged were reduced to the greatest straits. The supplies of food were carefully reserved for the fighting
men; the women and children, and all who could
not bear arms, were forced to support a miserable
existence on roots, shellfish, and even boiled leather.
At last the useless mouths were driven out, but the
king sternly refused to let them pass, and many
died of starvation between the walls and the royal

lines. Nothing but the iron resolution of the mayor,
Guiton, prevented an immediate surrender, when
the news came that Buckingham, just as he was
preparing to start for their relief, had fallen a
victim to Felton's knife. This event delayed the expedition, but it sailed in September under the command of the earl of Lindsay. It was now too late.
The two moles had been completed, and the gap
between them had not only been filled with sunken
vessels, but was also guarded night and day by a
number of ships fastened together in the shape of
a half-moon. The only chance was to make a
way through by means of fire-ships, which had
once been so successful at Antwerp. But the fire-
ships were ill-directed, and were grappled and
towed to shore by French boats. The English attack was a failure. Charles vainly tried to negotiate
on terms which might have been possible before
Buckingham's repulse from Rhé, but which were
preposterous now that the fall of La Rochelle was
inevitable. The citizens at last realised that their
cause was hopeless and on October 28 they agreed
to capitulate, on condition that their lives should
be spared, and liberty of worship allowed to them.
Richelieu's influence over the king was strong
enough to prevent the attack upon a rebellious

city from being converted into a crusade against heresy. Two days later the triumphal entry took place. The three marshals marched abreast to avoid any disputes as to precedence, then came the cardinal alone, and then the king. Richelieu appeared on that day as the first subject of France. On the city of La Rochelle fell the punishment from which the citizens were spared. Its walls were destroyed, its municipal privileges were cancelled, and no Protestant who had not been born there might take up his residence in the town. Even the fortresses of St. Louis and St. Martin were to be razed to the ground, as there was no longer any need for their existence.

Thus Richelieu had lived to achieve the scheme which he had dreamed of when he was simple bishop of Luçon. He had humbled the last municipality which was capable of resisting the power of the monarchy. To him, more than any other man, was the victory due, and his wise moderation had prevented its being abused in a way that would have produced lasting disaffection and disunion in France. The capture of La Rochelle was the achievement to which, in his later years, he looked back with the greatest pride and the most unalloyed satisfaction.

CHAPTER V

LA ROCHELLE had fallen but Casale was still holding out. It was not yet too late for Richelieu to resume that policy of opposition to Spain which the quarrel with England and the revolt of the Huguenots had compelled him for a time to abandon. He had allied himself with the Ultramontane party, but he was not their slave. To their intense disgust he again postponed the annihilation of Rohan and the Huguenots in the south, while he concentrated his attention upon the maintenance of French interests in Italy. The question of the Mantuan succession requires a few words of explanation.

Vincenzo di Gonzaga, who had succeeded two of his brothers as duke of Mantua and marquis of Montferrat, died without issue on December 26,

1627. His nearest male heir was Charles of Gonzaga, duke of Nevers, a French subject, and governor of the French province of Champagne. But though female succession was excluded in Mantua, it was lawful in Montferrat, and to prevent the separation of his territories, the late duke had married his niece, Mary, to Nevers's son, the duke of Rethel. In January 1628 the duke of Nevers took possession of his inheritance, to which his legal claim was unquestionable. But Spain, the dominant power in Italy, was determined to prevent the establishment of French influence within that country. Encouraged by the prospect of Spanish support, various claimants came forward to oppose the succession of the French duke. The duke of Guastalla, also a descendant of the Gonzagas, laid claim to Mantua on the ground that the Nevers family had forfeited its rights by having borne arms against the emperor. The duchess of Lorraine, sister of the three last dukes, maintained the legality of female succession in Montferrat, and Charles Emmanuel of Savoy advanced an old claim of his family to the same province. The emperor Ferdinand II., urged on by Spain, asserted his right as suzerain to settle these disputes, and in the meanwhile ordered the provinces to be handed over to his commissioner, John of Nassau.

The new duke of Mantua, trusting in support from France, refused to obey this order, and the Spaniards at once undertook to enforce the imperial authority. They were most immediately interested in Montferrat, which they regarded as a bulwark of the duchy of Milan. The alliance of Savoy was easily purchased by the promise of considerable territories in Montferrat, and Don Gonzales, governor of Milan, led an army to the siege of Casale, the chief fortress of the province. Nevers, hardly established in Mantua, could not hope to resist the combined forces of Spain and Savoy. France, occupied in the siege of La Rochelle, could not interfere effectually in Italy, and a small force which was sent under the marquis of Uxelles was repulsed at the entrance into Piedmont. Fortunately a small body of French volunteers had thrown themselves into the citadel of Casale, where the defective skill and vigilance of the besiegers enabled them to maintain themselves until the fall of La Rochelle set Richelieu and the royal army at liberty.

Although the season was extremely ill-suited for

such an enterprise, Richelieu determined to cross the Alps for the relief of Casale, and if possible to take the king with him. Mary de Medici, who cherished an old grudge against Nevers, and disapproved of the expedition altogether, did all in her power to induce her son to stay in Paris. But Louis XIII. had tasted the sweets of martial glory before La Rochelle, and the success of his arms had inspired him with enthusiastic confidence in the cardinal. On January 15, 1629, they quitted Paris together, and after travelling through Champagne they reached Grenoble on February 14. No other minister accompanied them, Schomberg having fallen ill at Troyes, and the whole burden of making preparations for the campaign fell upon Richelieu. The administrative system in the provinces was extremely corrupt and inefficient, and only the most authoritative supervision could secure that orders should be punctually carried out. But the cardinal's energy vanquished all obstacles, and on February 22 the king set out from Grenoble for the pass of Mont Genèvre. Charles Emmanuel sent his eldest son, who had married Louis's sister, to negotiate, but Richelieu discovered that the negotiations were merely intended to procure delay

while the intrenchments on the Italian side of the
pass were being strengthened. The order to advance
was given, and the French attack carried all before
it. The intrenchments were forced, and on March
3 the king entered Susa in triumph. This vigorous
action brought the duke of Savoy to reason, and
the prince of Piedmont was again sent to arrange
terms with Richelieu. The treaty of Susa was signed
on March 11. The duke promised to give the
French passage through his territories, and to
furnish supplies for the relief of Casale. As security
for the fulfilment of his promise Susa was to be
left in French occupation. He also undertook for
Don Gonzales that the Spaniards would retire from
Casale and Montferrat, that they would abstain
from any further acts of hostility against the duke
of Mantua, and that the confirmation of these
terms by Philip IV. should be obtained within six
weeks. Louis, on the other hand, promised to procure for the duke the town of Trino and other
lands in Montferrat to the value of 15,000 crowns,
as the price of the renunciation of his claims. At
the same time Richelieu drew up a projected league
for mutual defence between France, the pope,
Venice, Mantua, and Savoy. Charles Emmanuel

undertook to adhere to this league when it had been joined by the other states.

The prompt action of the French had thus secured for them a second military triumph within six months. The Spaniards could not hope to resist the royal army, and Don Gonzales was compelled to accept the terms which Charles Emmanuel had arranged for him. Casale was relieved, and there was yet plenty of time left to reduce the Huguenots. Louis XIII. set out from Susa in April to commence this task. Richelieu remained behind to watch the duke of Savoy, who was too veteran an intriguer to be trusted to fulfil his engagements of his own accord, but on May 19 the cardinal was able to join the king before Privas, the Protestant stronghold of the Vivarais. He had already dealt a crushing blow to the Huguenots by concluding a treaty with England. Charles I. abandoned the cause of the rebels, who had been led to rely upon English assistance, and Louis withdrew his demand for the restoration of Henrietta's household. Rohan, who had foreseen the defection of England, had sought compensation in an alliance with Spain, and the Most Catholic king had not hesitated to sign a treaty with the leader of Protestantism in France.

If any had been needed, this treaty would have supplied ample justification to Richelieu for his determination to crush the Huguenots. It provided that if they succeeded in forming an independent state, they would grant toleration to Roman Catholic worship. The possibility of such an ideal being entertained was enough to convince Richelieu that he must strike boldly and decisively if he wished to effect that unity of France which was the ultimate object of all his exertions.

Before Spanish assistance could arrive the blow had been struck. Privas was taken soon after Richelieu's arrival, and sacked with all the horrors of war. This severity, which the cardinal in his *Memoirs* maintains to have been unintentional, was as effective as if it had been deliberately planned. The Vivarais submitted, and the king entered the Cevennes, offering amnesty and toleration to all who submitted, and to those who resisted the fate of Privas. The alternative was irresistible, and one town after another opened its gates. The rebellion had collapsed, and the Huguenot deputies hastened to accept the terms which were offered to them, not as a treaty between equals, but as an act of grace from a sovereign to his subjects. The Edict of Nantes was confirmed, but the political privileges which had been granted at the same time by supplemental edicts were cancelled. The Huguenot fortifications were to be razed to the ground, and there were to be no more "towns of surety." Freedom of worship and of individual belief was granted, but it was granted as a royal favour which could at any time be revoked. Henry IV. had not been strong enough to enforce toleration by the royal authority, and had been forced to place weapons of self-defence in the hands of the Huguenots. Thanks to Richelieu, the monarchy could now afford to dispense with such precautions, and could thus revoke privileges which its own weakness had rendered necessary, and which had been used against itself. The danger of the formation of "a state within the state" was at an end. The only misfortune was that Richelieu could not ensure that the monarchy should always be tolerant.

After a triumphal entry into Nîmes, Louis XIII. set out for Paris on July 25. Richelieu remained behind to obtain the submission of Montauban, only second to La Rochelle as a Huguenot fortress, to supervise the destruction of the fortifications,

and to put an end to the administrative independence of Languedoc. It was not till September 14
that he was able to rejoin the king at Fontainebleau.
He soon found that he had to confront difficulties
at court quite as serious as those which he had
coped with abroad. Gaston of Orleans had never
been well disposed to Richelieu, whom he accused
of a deliberate scheme to exclude him from all voice
in public affairs. He was still the puppet of a small
group of interested associates, who wished to use
him as a catspaw for their own advancement. His
first wife had died in childbirth, and he was anxious
to marry Mary of Gonzaga, the daughter of the
duke of Mantua. This was opposed both by his
brother and mother; and Mary de Medici, during
the king's absence in Italy, went so far as to im-
prison the princess Mary at Vincennes. Gaston then
demanded an increase of his appanage, and the
government of some important provinces, such as
Champagne and Burgundy. Louis was so jealous
of his younger brother that Richelieu's advice was
not needed to convince him of the danger of hand-
ing over frontier provinces to a discontented heir-
apparent. Gaston, however, attributed the refusal
to the influence of the cardinal, and loudly de-

manded his dismissal. When Louis returned from Languedoc, Gaston refused to meet him at court, and retired to Champagne. There he professed to believe that he was in personal danger, and proceeded to Lorraine, where Charles IV., always willing to harass the French government, received him with open arms.

Still more formidable to Richelieu was the open hostility displayed to him on his arrival by Mary de Medici. For the last three years the relations of the queen-mother and her former servant had been growing more and more strained, and the chief cause of her ill-will are not difficult to trace. Throughout her life Mary de Medici was guided rather by passion than by policy. She cherished strong likes and dislikes, but they were directed against persons, not against principles. She had learnt to regard Richelieu as a creature of her own, who owed his advancement to her patronage, and she was chagrined to find him acting in complete independence of her wishes. She intended to keep her elder son entirely under her own control, and she discovered, to her dismay, that the cardinal's influence over Louis was stronger than her own. The guiding thread to the tortuous labyrinth of

her caprices is to be found in a steady attachment
to dynastic interests, and especially to those of her
three daughters.

This brought her into direct collision with the
cardinal's policy, which was dictated solely by a
regard to the interests of France. Her eldest daughter was the queen of Spain, and Richelieu was the
arch opponent of that power. Another daughter
was married into the house of Savoy, and Mary de
Medici would gladly have supported its claims to
Montferrat. But Richelieu had actually carried
Louis off to Piedmont, had humiliated the duke of
Savoy, and had forced him to resign his claims in
favor of the duke of Nevers, whom she hated, both
for his past career, and because he wished to become
the father-in-law of her younger son. The third
daughter was the wife of Charles I., and her interests—so her mother thought—had been completely
sacrificed in the last treaty with England. After
the interests of her family, Mary de Medici was
most solicitous for the interests of religion, and
these were specially urged upon her at this time
by her most intimate advisers, Cardinal Bérulle and
Michel Marillac. They wished for a general alliance
of Catholic against Protestant states, for the main-

tenance of a good understanding with Spain, and
for the persecution of the Huguenots at home. But
their aims were not those of Richelieu. If political
reasons rendered it advisable, he was as willing to
ally himself with Holland or Sweden as with
Bavaria or Austria. He had ample experience of
the hollowness of Spanish promises, and of the
resolution of the court of Madrid to do all in its
power to weaken France by stimulating internal
discord and encouraging foreign enemies. He may
also have been actuated by a sentiment of personal
rivalry against the Spanish minister, Olivares, who
certainly entertained that feeling towards Richelieu. Finally, he had reduced La Rochelle and
Languedoc, but Bérulle, a bigoted mystic, could
not pardon him for having left the heretics in enjoyment of religious toleration.

Against the hostility of the queen-mother, based
upon personal, dynastic, and religious motives,
Richelieu was not without supporters. Mary de
Medici, as in the days of her regency, had connected herself with the Guise party at court. Her
favourite confidant was the princess of Conti, a
sister of the duke of Guise. She made up her former
quarrel with her daughter-in-law, Anne of Austria,

also a vigorous hater of Richelieu, and opened a connection with the queen's exiled favourite, Madame de Chevreuse, whose husband was a Guise. The duke of Guise himself had a personal quarrel with Richelieu because he claimed the command in the Mediterranean as pertaining to his governorship of Provence, whereas the cardinal held that his office give him control over all maritime affairs in every sea. But the old antagonism between the Guises and the princes of the blood—a dominant factor in the history of the later part of the six-teenth century—still subsisted, and the cardinal could oppose to the queen's partisans the support of Condé, who had become his enthusiastic admirer since the siege of La Rochelle, and of the count of Soissons, who had now returned to France, and had made up his quarrel with the government. His only real security, however, lay in the hold which he had acquired over Louis XIII. Richelieu was no favourite, in the proper sense of the word. He did not rise to power, like Buckingham, by personal favour, nor did he retain it by flattering his master and humouring his foibles. But he was a favourite in the sense that every minister of a despotic sovereign must be a favourite. He could not hold his office if he forfeited the king's confidence or incurred his serious displeasure. Circumstances had brought him into Louis XIII.'s service, and he had so employed them as to make himself indispensable. Much has been written, in contemporary memoirs and in later histories, of the ascendency acquired by Richelieu over the king, and of the jealous hatred which Louis entertained against the minister, whose superiority he resented, but whom he dared not thwart or dismiss. Much of this can be proved by documentary evidence to be an exaggeration of the cardinal's enemies. Louis XIII. was rather timid than weak, and his moral cowardice made him eager to say what would please the person he was talking to. He was also slow and hesitating in his speech, and he was often unable to find words to answer the violent expostulations of his mother, or the voluble entreaties of his wife. His silence was easily interpreted to imply what he had no intention of expressing, for under his apparent weakness was concealed considerable obstinacy of opinion and purpose. He really shared his minister's devotion to the aggrandisement of France in Europe and the increased authority of the monarchy. Probably they often differed as to the means which were to be employed, and the cardinal's superior abilities doubtless enabled him as a rule to convince and persuade the king; but there were several occasions when Richelieu found it advisable to give way, and any temporary resentment which Louis may have entertained was more than removed by the success which attended their joint exertions. It is impossible to prove that Louis loved his minister, but he respected him, and he loved nobody.

The coldness with which the queen-mother received Richelieu at Fontainebleau was too obvious to escape the notice of a curious court. Richelieu met the hostility of his former patroness by offering his resignation—a favourite weapon in the hands of a minister conscious of his fidelity and of the merit of his services. Louis, who "wept bitterly for nearly a whole day" on account of his mother's importunities, refused to accept the resignation, and issued letters-patent conferring upon the cardinal the formal dignity of "principal minister of state." Mary de Medici was compelled to swallow her indignation, and she was the more willing to postpone her desire for vengeance as the death of Bérulle—whom Richelieu was absurdly accused of

poisoning—deprived her of one of her most trusted
advisers. Richelieu now set himself to arrange
terms with Gaston of Orleans, whose residence at
a foreign court was a glaring proof of French dissensions, and an encouragement to the enemies of
France. Months were wasted in the attempt to
satisfy the jealous prince and his ambitious councillors, and it was not till January 1630 that the
offer of an increased appanage induced Gaston to
return to France, though he still refused to see his
brother or to appear at court.

Meanwhile Richelieu discovered that he ran the
risk of losing all that he had achieved by his march
to Piedmont. The emperor, elated by his victories
over the German Calvinists and their Danish champion, was furious at the attempt of France to settle
the succession to imperial fiefs without any regard
to his authority. He looked on the treaty of Susa
as an insult, and withdrew a considerable number
of his troops from the north to vindicate his
suzerainty in Italy. In the spring of 1629 the imperial army entered the Grison territory and proceeded to occupy the Valtelline and other passes.
After some time had been spent in negotiations,
the imperial general, Colalto, descended into the

Lombard plain. Philip IV. and Olivares were eager
to seize the opportunity for resuming the schemes
which they had been forced for the moment to
abandon. The unconquered Spinola was sent to
supersede Don Gonzales in the government of
Milan. While the Imperialists advanced upon
Mantua, where the duke himself was shut up,
Spinola led the Spanish troops into Montferrat
and again threatened Casale, which was now defended by a French garrison under Toiras, the hero
of St. Martin.

France could not allow Spain and the empire to
triumph in Italy, and the despatch of a new army
was an obvious necessity. But who was to lead it?
The expedition involved diplomatic as well as
military difficulties, and their solution could not
safely be trusted to a subordinate. Richelieu, of
course, was anxious not to leave Louis XIII. to resist
unaided the influence and intrigues of Mary de
Medici and her partisans. On the other hand, he
could hardly venture once more to expose the still
childless king to the hardships and dangers of a
winter campaign. Moreover the treaty with Gaston
was not yet finally settled, and there was danger
of an attack from Germany on the side of Cham-

pagne. In the interests of France Richelieu was compelled to risk his personal security. On December 29, 1629, he set out from Paris with powers such as have rarely been granted to a subject. He was appointed "lieutenant-general, representing the person of the king with his army both within and without the kingdom." He had authority to receive and send envoys, and to conclude or reject treaties. Under him served Marshals Créqui, Schomberg, and la Force.

The passage of the Alps was effected without opposition, though not without considerable loss, and in the first week of March the French army reached Susa. Richelieu had made up his mind not only to fight the battles of the duke of Mantua, but also to secure some fortress at the foot of the Alps that would enable France at any time to interfere decisively in Italy. He had no intention of falling into the error of Louis XII. and Francis I., and of attempting to make France the mistress of Italian provinces, but he meant to strike a blow at Spanish domination, and to gain the confidence of those Italian states which still retained a shadow of independence. The great difficulty in his way was the attitude of Savoy. If Charles Emmanuel had been willing to fulfil the treaty of Susa, it would have been impossible to pick a quarrel with him, and it was only at his expense that the desired fortress could be acquired. But the wily duke played into the cardinal's hands. His one idea was to involve France and Spain in open hostilities with each other, and to make his own profit by selling his support to the highest bidder. He offered to aid the French, if they would join him in attacking Milan and Genoa, and would promise not to lay down arms till both had been conquered. This Richelieu refused, as he did not wish for an open rupture with Spain, and desired that France should continue to play the part of an auxiliary and not of a principal in the war. Then the duke offered to remain neutral, and to supply provisions for the French. This Richelieu at first accepted, in order that Casale might obtain ample supplies to resist a blockade. But he soon discovered that Charles Emmanuel was also negotiating with Spinola and Colalto, and that he was strengthening the intrenched camp which he had formed at Avigliana, between Susa and Turin, as a barrier against the French advance. Richelieu now decided to abandon negotiations, and to turn his arms against his treacherous ally, as it would be madness to advance upon Casale with a hostile Piedmont in his rear. On March 19 the French army advanced against Rivoli, where Charles Emmanuel had his headquarters. An eye-witness has described the cardinal's appearance as he crossed the little river Dora at the head of the troops. "He wore a blue cuirass over a brown coat embroidered with gold. He had a feather round his hat, and two pages marched before him on horseback, one carrying his gauntlets, the other his helmet. Two other pages marched on either side of him, and each held by the bridle a valuable charger; behind rode the captain of his guards. In this guise he crossed the river on horseback, with his sword at his side and two pistols at his saddle-bow. When he had reached the other side he made his horse caracole a hundred times in presence of the army, boasting aloud that he knew something of this exercise." In spite of all this martial pomp, the assault on Rivoli failed to effect the desired capture of the duke and his son, who escaped to Turin. But instead of advancing upon the capital of Piedmont, the French suddenly returned towards the Alps and invested Pinerolo, a fortress commanding the exit of the chief pass

from Dauphiné. Pinerolo, which had been held by
France for a considerable period in the previous
century, was compelled to surrender on March 30,
before the duke of Savoy had time to relieve it.

The capture of Pinerolo was a terrible blow, not
only to the duke of Savoy, but also to the Spaniards
and Imperialists, whose chief dread was that the
French might obtain a permanent footing in Italy.
They at once offered to negotiate, and Urban VIII.
undertook the office of mediator. It was on this
occasion that Giulio Mazarin, who was employed
as a papal agent, first attracted the notice of Richelieu, whose service he afterwards entered, and
whom he eventually succeeded as first minister in
France. The negotiations came to nothing, because
the one essential condition of peace was the cession
of Pinerolo, and Richelieu had no intention of
resigning his conquest except in the last necessity.
But so far he had done nothing for the duke of
Mantua, and Spinola and Colalto were already preparing to resume the sieges of Casale and Mantua,
which had been abandoned during the winter. The
cardinal conceived the bold plan of saving these
fortresses by an invasion of Savoy. If the Spaniards
and Imperialists advanced to the aid of their ally,

they would have to postpone their enterprises in Montferrat and Mantua. If they did not, the duke of Savoy would be compelled to come to terms, and this would render possible the despatch of an army to relieve Casale. If the worst came to the worst, and both Mantua and Casale fell, France would have something substantial in hand to offer in return for their restitution.

On May 2 Richelieu left the army at Pinerola under Schomberg and la Force, and hurried to Grenoble to meet Louis XIII., who had undertaken to conduct the invasion of Savoy. The king had started in the company of his mother and his wife, both of whom disapproved of the expedition, but he had left the two queens at Lyons. From Grenoble the king and cardinal advanced into Savoy, and their operations were conducted with the good-fortune which had always attended their joint presence. Chambéry surrendered after a siege of one day, and in June the wholy duchy had been reduced, with the exception of the single fortress of Montmélian. The natural sequel to this success was an advance to the relief of Casale, which was now closely besieged by Spinola. But the outbreak of pestilence in Piedmont made it impossible for

Louis XIII. to enter Italy, and Richelieu's position was now so directly threatened by the queen-mother and her adherents that he dared not risk another period of absence from the king. The bulk of the royal army was despatched on July 6 under Montmorency and d'Effiat across Mont Cenis, and they succeeded, after a sharp contest with the troops of Charles Emmanuel at Avigliana, in effecting a junction with the army which had been left at Pinerolo. The marquisate of Saluzzo was now conquered by the French, but their success was more than counterbalanced by the news that Mantua, which the Venetians had undertaken to relieve, had been stormed on July 17, and that the Imperialist forces were free to advance to the aid of Spinola. Charles Emmanuel, whose intrigues had resulted in the loss of the greater part of his dominions, died on July 26, but his successor, Victor Amadeus, though less committed to an anti-French policy, could not free himself at once from the obligations which his father bequeathed to him. France, therefore, gained nothing directly from the change of rulers. Meanwhile Casale was being hardly pressed, and Toiras announced that he could not hold out much longer without assistance. If

Richelieu could have come to Italy in person, the threatened fortress might have been relieved, but the cardinal was more than ever absorbed by the king's ill-health and the machinations of his enemies. In his absence, the French marshals were afraid to run the risk of a bold and decisive march, and their troops were harassed by sickness and bad weather. Under these circumstances Mazarin was at last able to arrange a truce at Rivalta on September 4. Hostilities were to be suspended on all sides until October 15; the town and castle of Casale were to be handed over to the besieging army, who were to supply provisions for the interval to the garrison of the citadel. After October 15, if peace had not been concluded, the French army might resume its advance, but Toiras pledged himself to surrender if relief did not reach him before October 30. Spinola, who was lying on his death-bed, refused to abandon his prey by signing the truce, but it was accepted by the duke of Savoy and Colalto, and the death of the veteran general three days later removed all difficulties, as his successor pledged himself to observe the stipulations.

It was fortunate for France, in its quarrel with the emperor and with Spain, that Richelieu had

not relied solely upon the achievements of the
French arms in Italy. His gaze embraced the whole
field of European politics, and he knew how to
make the most various and distant circumstances
subserve his immediate aims. It was the retirement
of Christian IV. of Denmark from the German
war which had enabled the emperor to send an
army against Mantua. But Richelieu had already
made preparations to bring another prince on the
stage to take the place vacated by the Danish king.
Gustavus Adolphus, the young and energetic king
of Sweden, had many motives for hostility to the
emperor, and he was eager to defend the cause of
Protestantism and to extend the power of Sweden
on the Baltic coasts. He had already thwarted
Wallenstein's attempt to take Stralsund, and nothing but his dynastic quarrel with the Polish king
prevented him from throwing himself into Germany. Here was Richelieu's opportunity. Early in
1629 a French envoy, Charnacé, had been despatched to the northern courts. He succeeded in
negotiating a ten years' truce between Poland and
Sweden, and he drew up a projected treaty of
alliance between Sweden and France. Thus Gustavus Adolphus was able to enter Germany in the

next year without leaving his own territories exposed to invasion, and with the additional advantage that a large contingent of the emperor's troops was engaged in Italy.

Still more skilful were the combinations of Richelieu's policy in Germany. The victories of Wallenstein had raised the power of the empire to a height which had not been reached for more than three centuries; but at the same time they had weakened the alliance between the emperor and the Catholic League. Maximilian of Bavaria and his associates had fought to humiliate the Protestants; but they had no intention of sacrificing their princely independence to the domination of Ferdinand II. and his haughty general. They demanded the dismissal of Wallenstein and the disbandment of his army. It was in vain that Ferdinand tried to conciliate them by issuing in 1629 an edict ordering the restitution of all ecclesiastical possessions which had been occupied by Protestants since the great religious peace of Augsburg. The only result was to alienate the Lutheran princes, who had been the most loyal adherents of the empire, and who were forced against their will to form an alliance with Sweden. The Catholics continued to persist in their demands, and their opposition, carefully stimulated by Richelieu, brought matters to a crisis at the diet of Ratisbon, which Ferdinand summoned in June 1630, to procure the election of his son as king of the Romans. Richelieu sent Leon de Brulart as French ambassador to the diet, and with him went the cardinal's *alter ego,* the famous Father Joseph. Their intrigues were crowned with complete success. At the moment when Gustavus Adolphus landed on the coast of Pomerania, Ferdinand was compelled to dismiss Wallenstein and to hand over his army to Tilly, the general of the Catholic League. Even at this price he was unable to obtain his son's election, which Richelieu had instructed his envoys to oppose.

The emperor, deprived of his German army and his greatest general, was no longer able to continue the war in Italy. The Catholic princes had always been opposed to the war, and they were eager to bring about peace with France, which they had learnt to regard as their ally. On October 13 Father Joseph and his colleague signed the treaty of Ratisbon, which was to settle the question of the Mantuan succession. The dukes of Savoy and Guastalla were to receive compensation for the resignation of their claims; the emperor was to give formal investiture to the duke of Mantua within six weeks, and a fortnight after the investiture had been granted the Imperialists were to quit Mantua, the Spaniards Montferrat, and the French their conquests in Savoy and Piedmont. After all this had been done the emperor was to withdraw his forces from the Grison passes and to destroy the newly-erected fortifications. France pledged herself to give no assistance, direct or indirect, to the enemies of the emperor. Copies of the treaty were at once dispatched to the court at Lyons and to the French camp in Italy.

It is extremely improbable that Father Joseph acted in this matter in opposition to Richelieu's instructions, and it is certain that he never forfeited the cardinal's favour or confidence. But Richelieu clamoured that the envoys had exceeded their powers, and that the treaty was so disadvantageous to France that it could not possibly be confirmed. The solution of the problem seems to be that Father Joseph was playing a preconcerted part at Ratisbon.

At all costs he was to conciliate the Catholic electors to France and to prevent the election of a king of the Romans. These ends he could only ob-

tain by signing the treaty. But Richelieu had so
worded the instructions of his representatives as to
reserve to himself the power of rejecting the terms
which they had found it advisable to accept. And it
is possible that events at home made the prompt
conclusion of peace at this moment peculiarly un-
acceptable to him. The health of Louis XIII. had
suffered from the hot weather in Savoy. The solici-
tations of his mother induced him to return to
Lyons, and there he was seized with an attack of
dysentery, which was aggravated by the exhausting
treatment then in vogue. As his doctor bled him
seven times in a week, and administered an innumerable variety of drugs, it is no wonder that his life
was despaired of. The crisis to which Richelieu must
often have looked forward seemed to have arrived
on September 20, when the king received extreme
unction and took a formal farewell of the world.
Gaston of Orleans prepared to succeed to his
brother's crown, if not, as some say, to his brother's
wife. The enemies of the cardinal discussed who
should take his place, and whether it was better to
remove him by imprisonment or by death. Their
schemes were suddenly disconcerted by the king's
recovery; but in the exhaustion of convalescence he

gave way to the incessant pressure of his wife and his mother, and held out hopes that he would dismiss the cardinal as soon as peace was concluded. The king's promise was not very definite; but the mere suspicion of such an intention was enough to make Richelieu insist upon the defects of the treaty of Ratisbon.

Meanwhile the news of this treaty reached the French camp just as the army was advancing to effect the relief of Casale before October 30. Montmorency had been recalled to France, and his place was taken by Louis Marillac, brother of the keeper of the seals, who had previously commanded the army of Champagne. He wished to accept the terms, but his colleagues, Schomberg and d'Effiat, insisted that they were too favourable to the enemy. By the truce of Rivalta the Spaniards were to quit Casale as soon as the citadel had been relieved, whereas by the treaty they would be allowed to remain there for two months. The march was resumed, and on October 27 the two armies were on the point of an engagement, when Mazarin appeared between them at the imminent risk of being shot for his pains, and announced that peace had been arranged. The Spaniards agreed to quit

Montferrat at once, on condition that Casale was handed over to the duke of Maine, the son of the duke of Mantua, who was to pledge himself to maintain only a native garrison in the citadel. The French had so far triumphed that Casale had never been taken, and that they retained their conquests in Savoy and Piedmont as security for the evacuation by the Imperialists of Mantua and the Valtelline.

The news of the relief of Casale reached the French court as it was returning from Lyons to Paris after the king's recovery, and Mary de Medici had a bonfire kindled to celebrate the event. She believed that the Italian difficulty was at an end, and that Louis would now dismiss the hated minister, whom he no longer needed. To her astonishment the king opposed an obstinate resistance to her entreaties, refused to recognise any engagements made during his illness, and desired his mother to abandon her ill-founded enmity against the cardinal. At last Mary's passion got the better of the crafty dissimulation which was the tradition of her family. On November 10 she picked a violent quarrel, in the king's presence, with Madame de Combalet, the cardinal's favourite niece. After up-

braiding her in language that would have disgraced
a fishwife, she bade her leave her service and presence for ever. The king himself escorted the young
woman, weeping and scared by such an unexpected
scene, to the door, which was soon afterwards entered by the uncle. Mary de Medici turned her fury
upon him with the same vehemence of language
and gesticulation. Richelieu made no attempt to
defend himself, but listened in respectful silence,
and quitted the room. Then the queen turned to
her son: she accused the cardinal of designing to
marry his niece to the count of Soissons, to depose
Louis, and to place the count on the throne.

Forgetting that she supplied evidence of a preconcerted conspiracy, she divulged her schemes for
the conduct of the government after Richelieu's
fall. Michel Marillac was to become chief minister,
and his brother was to assume the supreme command of the army. The king made no attempt to
interrupt or reply to this violent monologue. He
retired to his chamber and threw himself in a rage
upon his bed. He was unwilling to quarrel irretrievably with his mother, but he had no intention
of parting with his minister. The very complaints
which he had listened to only furnished a striking

proof of Richelieu's fidelity. The basis of the queen-
mother's resentment was that the cardinal was more
devoted to the king than to herself. Louis's cham-
berlain and favourite, St. Simon, father of the
famous memoir-writer, strengthened his resolution
by urging that he had duties not only as a son, but
also as a king, and that the cardinal was necessary
to France. To escape any further maternal intimi-
dation, the king determined to depart for Versailles.

Meanwhile Mary de Medici had convinced herself that her son's silence implied acquiescence. The
news of her victory was circulated through Paris,
and couriers were sent to announce the cardinal's
downfall to foreign courts. The French courtiers
crowded to the queen-mother's magnificent palace,
the Luxembourg, to offer their congratulations. The
rumour spread that Richelieu was collecting his
papers and valuables, and was preparing to depart
from Paris, if not from France. And it is true that
the cardinal was profoundly discouraged. He knew
how a violent woman may influence, in spite of
himself, a man who dislikes to have troubles and
displeasure around him. He may well have feared
that Mary de Medici's estimate of her success was
no exaggeration. While he thus desponded and hesi-

tated as to his future course, a messenger arrived
to bid him join the king at Versailles. Louis had
never really doubted as to his ultimate decision; he
was conscious that his reign owed its success and its
reputation to the cardinal; and if he had to choose
between his mother and his minister, his mind was
already made up. He only waited till he was safe
from interference to announce his determination.
On the next day Michel Marillac was called upon to
surrender the great seals, and a courier was despatched to Schomberg ordering him to arrest Marshal Marillac and to send him a prisoner to France.
November 11, 1630, has come down to history as
the "day of dupes."

Richelieu's position was all the stronger for the
failure of the attack upon him. Mary de Medici
was compelled to acknowledge her defeat, and in
December she controlled her rage so far as to be
formally reconciled with the cardinal, and to resume her seat in the council. But she had no intention of abandoning her desire for vengeance on the
man who had thwarted and humiliated her. As open
violence had failed, she determined to try once more
the paths of intrigue. Her elder son had escaped
from her influence, but she still had some control

over his younger brother. Gaston's importance as heir-apparent to the throne was far greater than his own abilities would have given him, and he was readily induced to fall in with his mother's wishes. In January 1631 he appeared in the cardinal's chamber and openly renounced his friendship; directly afterwards he set out for Orleans. It was the intention of the queen-mother to rally round her second son all the elements of opposition to the monarchy, and, if necessary, to trust to the chances of a civil war. Richelieu fully appreciated her designs. To allow her to remain in impunity at court would only strengthen and encourage her faction, and the king was easily persuaded to separate himself from an influence which he now dreaded and disliked. The court journeyed to Compiègne, and the queen-mother followed to watch her son. Early in the morning of February 23 the king and the cardinal hurried back to Paris. Anne of Austria was ordered to follow her husband, but was allowed to take a tender farewell of her mother-in-law, with whom she had been closely united of late years by common antipathy to Richelieu. They never met again. Mary de Medici received written instructions to retire for a time to Moulins, as circumstances made her presence at court undesirable. The princess of Conti and other ladies of her household were exiled to their estates, and Marshal Bassompierre, an ally of the Marillacs, was committed to a prison from which he never emerged while Richelieu lived.

The cardinal now tried to conciliate Gaston, but the prince was persuaded by his followers to reject all offers, and in March he retired for a second time to Lorraine. Meanwhile Mary de Medici obstinately refused to leave Compiègne, and endeavoured to excite sympathy by representing that she was harshly imprisoned by the man whom she had raised to greatness. Her residence so near to Paris was a constant source of annoyance to the king and minister, but they did not venture to risk unpopularity by removing her by force. Their end was at last effected by relaxing the careful watch hitherto maintained over her movements. Weary of inaction, the queen escaped from France in July, and made her way to Brussels. She was destined never to revisit the country in which her marriage had enabled her to play so prominent a part.

These exciting events had distracted public attention from the Mantuan question, which had so long absorbed it. Hostilities had been terminated by the truce concluded by Mazarin before Casale, but as Richelieu had steadily refused to confirm the treaty of Ratisbon, no permanent settlement had been agreed to. Early in 1631 the French envoys, Toiras and Servien, proceeded to Cherasco in Piedmont to meet the plenipotentiaries of the emperor, and the representatives of Spain, Savoy, and Mantua. The chief difficulties arose about the compensation to be given to the duke of Savoy for the resignation of his claims, and about the dates at which the various powers were to abandon their conquests. At length everything was settled by two treaties, in April and June, and in July the duke of Nevers received the imperial investiture of Mantua and Montferrat. To the surprise of contemporaries, it was the duke of Mantua who had most reason to be dissatisfied with the treaties of Cherasco. His champion, France, compelled him to sell the greater part of Montferrat to the duke of Savoy. The explanation was not long a secret. Richelieu publicly agreed to restore Pinerolo in order to satisfy European opinion and to obtain peace. But he was determined to keep the fortress if any opportunity offered. Victor Amadeus, instructed by the failure of his father's policy, was inclined to the French alliance which his marriages rendered natural. The offer of large territories in Montferrat induced him to consent that the French should have Pinerolo, and a secret treaty to that effect was signed on March 31. The only difficulty that remained was to obtain some plausible pretext for breaking the treaty of Cherasco, which stipulated for the restoration of all French conquests. Richelieu was not at a loss for an expedient. He complained that Spain kept so large a garrison in Milan as to excite the fear of a new attack on Mantua, and he called upon Savoy to give surety against any new league with the Spaniards. Victor Amadeus, after feigning an appeal for aid to Milan, agreed that Pinerolo should be handed over as a pledge, nominally to the Swiss, but in reality to the French. In 1632 this flimsy pretence was abandoned, and Pinerolo was bought by France.

Thus Richelieu had achieved a complete triumph in these years. He had obtained the submission of the Huguenots; he had defeated the intrigues and the open assaults of his domestic enemies; he had humbled Spain and the empire; and he had secured French influence in Italy by seating a Frenchman in the duchy of Mantua, and by obtaining for France the key of the Alpine passes.

CHAPTER VI

Louis XIII. was not ungrateful to the minister who in seven years had already done enough to make the reign notable in the history of France. In August 1631 he issued letters-patent creating Richelieu duke and peer. On September 5 the ceremony took place of admitting the new peer to the parliament. Condé, Montmorency, and the chief nobles of France formed his escort, but such a crowd had assembled at the doors that the procession could only make its way to the grand chamber through the galleries. Richelieu was never popular, but the people appreciated the grandeur of his aims and his achievements. They admired, if they did not love. At the same time the cardinal received the government of Brittany, so important for his maritime and commercial projects. Nor was it at home only

that his merits were applauded. The Republic of
Venice, always eager to recognise greatness outside
her own walls, sent a special envoy to offer him the
rank of noble, with power to name any of his relatives as his successor.

But no one knew better than Richelieu that he
was only on the threshold of greater difficulties
than those which he had already overcome. The
triumph of French policy in Italy had provoked
and alarmed the house of Hapsburg. Both Austria
and Spain were now fully alive to the danger which
threatened them if France, united at home, were to
espouse the cause of their enemies in Germany and
the United Provinces. Such a catastrophe could
only be prevented by doing all in their power to revive the embers of dissension in France. Spain was
the more immediately interested in this because the
line of provinces through which a connection was
maintained between Lombardy and the Netherlands ran along the eastern frontier of France. If
the emperor could only crush the opposition in
Germany, Spain would be free to suppress its dangerous rival in the west, and the means for attaining
this end were sufficiently obvious. The heir to the
French crown was more dangerous outside France

than he could be within. With the assistance of
foreign troops, and the support of the discontented
nobles and parliaments of his own country, Gaston
might succeed in overthrowing the minister whom
his favourites had taught him to detest. And with
the fall of Richelieu France might again become as
powerless and contemptible as it had been under the
regency of Mary de Medici.

The headquarters of the conspiracy were at
Nancy, where Gaston had taken refuge. Charles IV.
of Lorraine was eager to free his duchy from the
control which France had secured by the seizure in
1552 of the three bishoprics of Metz, Toul, and
Verdun. He had already raised an army of 15,000
men, and he had persuaded the emperor to enforce
his suzerainty over the three bishoprics by the capture of Moyenvic, a disputed dependency. With the
assistance of troops from the Netherlands and from
Germany, Lorraine might be a formidable starting-
point for an invasion of France. Gaston was to be
bound to the confederacy by a marriage with the
duke's sister, Margaret.

But Richelieu was far too prompt to allow his
enemies to complete their preparations. In the
winter of 1631 he despatched la Force and Schom-

berg to drive the Imperialists from Moyenvic, while
he carried off the king and court to Metz, leaving
Soissons as lieutenant-governor in Paris. Complete
success rewarded both movements, Moyenvic was
taken, and the duke of Lorraine hastened to conclude the Treaty of Vic (January 6, 1632), by
which he promised to withdraw from all hostile
alliances, and to expel from his territories all the
enemies of France. Richelieu hoped by depriving
Gaston of his refuge to induce him to accept a
reconciliation, but the latter was persuaded by his
chief adviser, Puylaurens, to withdraw to Brussels.
The plot was postponed and not abandoned.
Charles IV. had no intention of observing the
promises, and almost at the moment of the conclusion of the treaty of Vic Gaston was secretly married to Margaret of Lorraine.

While Richelieu was engaged in averting the immediate perils which threatened France, events were
occurring in Germany which were destined not
only to frustrate the schemes of his enemies, but to
open the way for a new policy of aggrandisement
and annexation. In 1632 the cardinal began to
dream of that extension of the French frontier to
the Rhine which becomes so dominant a tradition

in subsequent generations. The beginning of this great enterprise was one of the many important results of the victories of Gustavus Adolphus. Although the Swedish king had been urged by Richelieu to invade Germany, and although a formal treaty between them was concluded at Bärwalde in January 1631, the aims of the two great protagonists were far from harmonious. For the chief objects of Gustavus, the aggrandisement of Sweden and the maintenance or extension of Protestantism, Richelieu cared not at all. To him the Swedish army was merely a tool to be used for the humiliation of the house of Hapsburg, and to divert the attention of Austria from Italy and France. He would have preferred to attain his ends by an alliance with the Catholic League, if that had been possible, and it was only when he found that Maximilian of Bavaria had too many interests in common with the emperor that he finally decided on a treaty with Sweden. And his diplomacy, skilful as it was, was insufficient to keep a man like Gustavus Adolphus in the leading-strings of France. The latter set himself to secure his position in the north before he would risk a direct attack upon the enemies whom he had come to seek. The emperor's obstinate persistence in enforcing the Edict of Restitution drove the Lutheran princes into an alliance with Sweden. The hesitation of John George of Saxony, averse to the intervention of a foreigner in German affairs, and still more unwilling to acknowledge a superior, was finally overcome by the sack of Magdeburg. Having at last achieved his first aim, Gustavus Adolphus advanced to meet the army of the League under Tilly. Few more important battles have been fought than that of Leipzig (September 7, 1631). On its issue were staked the maintenance of Protestanism in Germany, the very existence of Sweden as a state, and in a lesser degree the future of France and its great minister. If Tilly had triumphed, it would have been immensely difficult to resist the foreign coalition in favour of Gaston of Orleans.

The victory of Gustavus Adolphus removed this danger, but the attention of Europe was at once concentrated upon the conqueror's future movements. If he marched straight upon Vienna, it seemed impossible that the emperor, without either army or general, could make any effective resistance, and terms of peace might be dictated in the capital of the Austrian Hapsburgs. This seemed the most obvious policy, and it had much to recom-

mend it to Richelieu, who had always desired to
employ the Swedes against Austria and to spare
the Catholic League. But Gustavus Adolphus was
jealous of French dictation, and resolute to follow
his own course. Leaving John George to invade Bohemia, he led his own army against the defenceless
states of the Rhine prelates. No resistance was
offered to his triumphal march, and before the end
of the year Mainz itself was in his hands. That
Richelieu was chagrined by his decision is un-
deniable. In his *Memoirs* he asserts that Gustavus
Adolphus, like Hannibal, knew how to conquer,
but not how to use his victory.

But in spite of the cardinal's criticism it is doubtful whether France could have been better served
by a direct attack upon Vienna than she was by
Gustavus's triumphal march along the "priests'
lane." The European coalition in favor of Gaston,
which depended more upon Spain than upon
Austria, was practically annihilated. The duke of
Lorraine was deprived of the allies who might have
interfered to protect him from the consequences of
his continued intrigues, and of his treacherous
breach of the treaty of Vic. But the chief result was
to give an opening for French intervention in

Southern Germany. The ecclesiastical electors
hastened to implore the mediation of the cardinal,
and the archbishop of Trier promptly placed himself under French protection, and offered to admit
French garrisons into his fortress of Hermanstein
(now Ehrenbreitstein) and Philipsburg. The marquis de Brézé, Richelieu's brother-in-law, was sent
to warn Gustavus Adolphus from a further advance
into Elsass, and to negotiate terms for the neutrality
of Bavaria and Cologne.

In order to profit by the opportunity which the
Swedish successes offered to him, Richelieu determined to make himself master of Lorraine, an
enterprise for which the conduct of Charles IV.
offered a convenient pretext. Gaston, after collecting troops in Brussels, had returned to Lorraine on
his way to France, where his emissaries were active
in stirring up the malcontent nobles to active
measures against the cardinal. As a warning to his
enemies, Richelieu brought Marshal Marillac to trial
for peculation before a special commission, and he
was condemned and executed (May 8). Richelieu
then recalled the French army, which had already
appeared on the Rhine and occupied Ehrenbreitstein, and carried the king with him to Lorraine. In

eight days the campaign was over. The capture of
Pont-à-Mousson, and the advance of Marshal d'Effiat to lay siege to Nancy, brought the duke to his
knees. By the treaty of Liverdun (June 26) he
undertook to observe the promises he had made at
Vic, to do homage for his duchy of Bar, and to sell
the county of Clermont to France. As security for
his good faith he was to leave his brother, the cardinal of Lorraine, as a hostage, and to place the
fortresses of Stenay and Jametz in French hands.
The French army was now free to renew the campaign in Germany, and, in spite of the discouragement caused by the death of d'Effiat, his successor,
d'Estrées, succeeded in driving the Spaniards from
the city of Trier. By thus seizing the bridge over
the Moselle, the French cut off the most direct route
between the Netherlands and the Spanish provinces
in Italy.

Having drawn the teeth of the duke of Lorraine,
it was now high time for Richelieu to turn his
attention to Gaston, who had entered France on
June 8, and had issued a manifesto containing a
violent attack upon the cardinal. Personally the
heir to the throne was a contemptible antagonist,
but he had succeeded in gaining over the greatest

noble in France, after the princes of the royal blood. Henri de Montmorency, the last bearer of a famous name in history, had won reputation as a soldier at Avigliana, and had since been on terms of affectionate intimacy with Richelieu, who relied on his fidelity. But the young duke was discontented with the humble part which the great nobles had to play under the cardinal's rule. He coveted his ancestors' office of constable, which had been suppressed, and he resented the harsh treatment of his province of Languedoc. Above all, the influence of his wife, a relative of Mary de Medici, urged him to come forward as the champion of the oppressed mother and brother of the king. He invited Gaston to advance from Burgundy into Languedoc, and it was confidently hoped that his name and reputation would give the rebels a firm footing in Southern France. But Richelieu was now to reap the reward of his firm and prudent policy. The Huguenots, contented with religious toleration, refused to join a movement which was encouraged by Spain. The chief nobles and governors of provinces, warned by the fate of Marillac, hesitated to commit themselves until some substantial success had been obtained, and the leaders of the rising were at variance among themselves. Puylaurens, eager to maintain his ascendency over the feeble Gaston, was jealous of Montmorency's influence, and the latter's claim to command was disputed by d'Elbœuf. These dissensions had already assured the failure of the rebels when they came into collision with the royal army under Schomberg at Castelnaudari (September 1). A chivalrous but reckless cavalry charge carried Montmorency into the middle of the enemy; his horse was killed under him, and he was carried from the field wounded and a prisoner.

Gaston, who accepted the devotion of his adherents without sharing their risks, and who had taken no part in the battle, at once realised that all was lost, and opened negotiations with Louis. There was no disposition to treat him harshly, and he received most lenient terms from his brother. On condition of abandoning all hostile alliances, he recovered all his appanages, and an amnesty was promised to most of his adherents, with the significant exception of Montmorency. Richelieu knew how to be moderate in the hour of victory. The king presided in person at a meeting of the estates of Languedoc at Béziers, and restored for a money payment the liberties of which the province had been deprived in 1629.

Attention was now concentrated upon the fate
of Montmorency, who had been basely deserted by
his accomplices, but whose life was pleaded for by
illustrious relatives, and even by crowned heads.
Richelieu, however, merciful as he had been to the
mass of the rebels, was determined to make an
example of their leader. He would teach the French
nobles that rebellion, even in the interests of the
heir to the throne, was not an enterprise to be
lightly undertaken. To the king he urged that
Montmorency's execution was the only way to
make Gaston powerless by depriving him of adherents. A still more potent argument to himself was
to be found in a remark made by Bullion, and
which is reproduced by the cardinal himself—that
the house of Montmorency was so powerful in
Languedoc that the people regarded the royal
power as imaginary. To Richelieu, the duke's removal may well have seemed an almost necessary
step to that absorption of the provinces under a
powerful monarchy and a centralised administration which was the grand object of his life. In his
Memoirs he pleads, not without plausibility, that
his severity proved his devotion to France at the
expense of his own personal interests. To have
spared the prisoner would have been an easy method

of gaining popularity. To punish him was to expose
his own life to the risk of assassination, because it
would convince his enemies that they could only
secure themselves by his death. But these considerations had little weight with Richelieu, who was
superior to vulgar terrors, and who had assimilated,
either consciously or unconsciously, the maxim of
Machiavelli, that it is safer to be feared than to be
loved. Montmorency was brought to trial before the
parliament of Toulouse, whose competence to pass
judgment on a peer was more than doubtful, condemned to death, and executed on the same day
(October 30). Men to whom the traditions of the
civil wars were still familiar, and who remembered
the impunity with which princes and nobles con-
spired under the regency, must have realised that
a new era had begun for France when a minister
of the crown ventured to bring to the scaffold the
last male of a family whose name was so honourably
and conspicuously written in the country's history.

One result of the execution Richelieu had probably failed to foresee. Although Gaston had omitted
to stipulate for Montmorency's pardon, even his
torpid selfishness could not but feel the ignominy
which the fate of his chivalrous supporter threw

upon himself. His own fears and those of Puy-laurens were kindled by the recollection that his marriage with Margaret of Lorraine had not yet been acknowledged, and that it would never be tolerated by the king and cardinal. On November 6 he fled from Tours, and again sought refuge in Brussels.

Thus the heir to the throne was once more in the hands of the enemies of France, and the task of depriving them of this dangerous weapon had to be commenced afresh. At the same time an event occurred in Germany which altered the whole aspect of affairs in Europe, and demanded the exercise of all Richelieu's prudent watchfulness. Gustavus Adolphus had listened to French remonstrances so far as to abstain from advancing into Elsass and to respect the neutrality of Trier. But he refused to resign the ecclesiastical territories which he had already seized, and the attempt to arrange terms with the leaders of the Catholic League proved a failure. Early in 1632 the Swedes advanced against Bavaria, and Tilly was defeated and slain in attempting to dispute the passage of the Lech. Gustavus Adolphus entered Munich in triumph, and Maximilian was driven from his own duchy.

Austria was once more exposed to invasion, and the army of the League was no longer able to defend the emperor. In his despair Ferdinand II. had been compelled to appeal to Wallenstein, who recovered his command on terms which made him an independent potentate. With an army which was brought together by the magic of his reputation, and which he treated as his private following, Wallenstein had already driven the Saxons from Bohemia, and he now advanced to check the eastward march of the Swedes. At Nürnberg Gustavus Adolphus met with his first check, as he dared not attack the enemy's intrenchments, and failed to force him into a pitched battle. From Nürnberg Wallenstein drew the Swedes after him into Saxony, and on November 16 their heroic king lost his life on the glorious field of Lützen.

At this very moment Richelieu was lying on a bed of sickness, from which it seemed more than possible that he would never rise again. After settling affairs in Languedoc, Louis XIII. had hurried back to Paris, while the cardinal undertook to escort the queen on a tour through Western France, where she was to visit his home at Richelieu and his great conquest, La Rochelle. But an internal abscess had long preyed upon a frame that had never been strong, and to this disorder was now added disease of the bladder. The cardinal was compelled to stop at Bordeaux, and to leave the task of entertaining Anne of Austria to his uncle, the commander de la Porte. About November 20 his condition seemed almost hopeless, and in Paris the rumour spread that he was dead. Open enemies and faithless friends exulted over the expected removal of an oppressor or a too-powerful patron. Châteauneuf, the keeper of the seals, who owed his elevation to Richelieu, was indiscreet enough to betray his hopes of succeeding to the position of his dying colleague. But an indomitable spirit often triumphs over the weakness of its mortal covering. Richelieu recovered as if by a miracle, and as soon as he had rejoined the court he hastened to punish those personal affronts which in his eyes were almost as unpardonable as serious crimes against the state. Châteauneuf was accused, on the loose assertions of the cardinal's spies, of being engaged in an intrigue with the duchess of Chevreuse, the queen-mother, and Henrietta Maria of England. His real offence was that he had deserted Richelieu at Bordeaux, that he had danced before the queen while his patron was

thought to be dying, and that he had allowed himself to dream of succeeding to the office of first
minister. For this he was deprived of the seals and
imprisoned at Angoulême, but the fact that he was
never brought to trial goes far to prove that there
was little foundation for the graver charges against
him.

Richelieu's recovery was exceedingly opportune,
as he found France threatened by three simultaneous dangers. The death of Gustavus Adolphus
weakened the league against the Austrian Hapsburgs, and might easily lead to its dissolution. The
United Provinces were negotiating for a truce with
Spain, and if this were arranged, the Spaniards
would be free to carry out their schemes for assist-
ing Gaston, who had again joined the enemies of his
country. Never did the cardinal display more coolness and decision than at this crisis, when the whole
weight of affairs rested on his own shoulders. His
colleagues in the council, of whom the chief were
Bullion and Bouthillier, had one great qualification
—devotion to their chief. They were always consulted by him, but the decision he always reserved
to himself, and they were quite content to carry
out a policy which they knew themselves to be in-

capable of originating. The only personage who may have possessed influence over Richelieu was Father Joseph, who was not officially a member of the council, and whose relations with the cardinal have always been something of an enigma to historians. Such evidence as we possess, however, goes to prove that the influence of the "grey cardinal" has been exaggerated by Richelieu's detractors, and that the special subjects on which he was consulted were affairs in Germany and the relations with Rome. Louis XIII. himself, whose penetration and decision the cardinal is never tired of contrasting with his own "simplicity," was conspicuously devoid of the qualities which his minister attributes to him. His notes on the minutes of the council, which are published in the great collection of M. d'Avenel, proved that he never dreamed of disputing the conclusions of an adviser whose superiority he always recognised even when he was most inclined to resent it.

Early in 1633 two of the ablest of French diplomatists, Feuquières and Charnacé, were despatched to Germany and Holland, and their instructions, which are model state-papers, show how clearly Richelieu comprehended the situation, and how he planned to turn it to the advantage of France.

While avoiding as long as possible an open declaration of war, he wished to strengthen all the elements of opposition to the house of Hapsburg, and to seize every opportunity for strengthening the monarchy at home and for extending the power of France on the eastern frontier. In Germany the embassy of Feuquières was completely successful. The alliance of France with Sweden, which was now governed by Oxenstiern on behalf of Christina, the young daughter of Gustavus, was renewed. At Heilbronn the influence of the French envoy was mainly instrumental in securing the confirmation of the Protestant League, which was strengthened by further additions at the later conference at Frankfurt. French diplomacy defeated the attempt of John George of Saxony to procure the direction of the League, which was given to Oxenstiern, but, to his great disgust, with strictly limited powers. Richelieu had regarded the death of Gustavus with composure, if not with secret complacency, and events justified his view. The Swedish king was an unmanageable ally, and continued successes might have enabled him to found a power independent of, and possibly formidable to, France. His removal rendered the Swedes again dependent upon French support, and at the same time enabled French influence gradually to supplant that of Sweden in Germany.

In Holland Charnacé was equally successful. By making dexterous use of the divisions among the seven provinces he succeeded in frustrating the negotiations with the Netherlands, where the Spanish power suffered a severe blow by the death of the popular and prudent infanta, Clara Isabella. The continuance of the Dutch war prevented the Spaniards from sending assistance to Charles IV. of Lorraine, who had been encouraged by the death of the Swedish king to disregard the obligations he had contracted at Liverdun. This gave Richelieu the opportunity which he wanted for the annexation of a province whose possession would be as advantageous as its hostility was dangerous to France. He had already employed the labours of learned antiquarians to prove that the imperial suzerainty was a usurpation which no lapse of time could legalise, and that Lorraine was properly a dependency of the French crown. Fortified with their arguments, he proceeded to take active measures. On the ground that the stipulated homage had never been paid for Bar, the parliament of Paris declared the

duchy confiscated. Saint Chaumont was sent with
an army to advance upon Nancy, and in August
Richelieu set out with the king to direct operations
on the spot. Charles IV., as unprepared as ever to
resist invasion, sent his brother, the cardinal of Lorraine, to offer to annul the marriage between Gaston and Margaret, and to propose on his own behalf
a marriage with Madame de Combalet. Richelieu
refused the proffered honour to his niece, and demanded that Nancy should be surrendered as a
pledge of the duke's good faith. As this condition
was rejected as too harsh, the French laid siege to the
capital of Lorraine, which was regarded as one of the
best fortresses of Europe. Charles IV. now gave way,
and agreed to surrender Nancy, but he still hoped
for the arrival of Spanish troops from Italy, and
ordered the commander of the citadel to delay the
formal cession. But the duke of Feria, who had already marched from Milan through the Valtelline,
was delayed at Constance by the Swedes under count
Horn. This check deprived Charles of his last hope,
and on September 25 Richelieu accompanied Louis
in his formal entry into Nancy. He was provided
beforehand with an excuse for retaining a pledge
which he had no intention of relinquishing. During

the siege the Princess Margaret, with the conni-
vance of her brothers, had escaped from the city
to Luxemburg, whence she proceeded to join her
husband in Brussels. Earlier in the year the creation
of a parliament at Metz had cut off the last link between the three bishoprics and the empire. The lilies
supplanted the imperial eagle, and the duchy of
Lorraine, with all its chief fortresses garrisoned by
French troops, was practically a province of France.
It was in vain that Charles IV. sought to disarm
the enmity of Louis by abdicating in favour of his
brother, who resigned the cardinalate and married
his cousin Claude. France refused to recognise the
marriage, and the new duke and his bride found
themselves compelled to escape imprisonment by
flying to Florence. Their departure enabled Richelieu to complete the occupation of Lorraine by
seizing the last fortresses and by establishing a *conseil souverain* at Nancy for the administration of
justice.

Although Margaret of Lorraine had escaped,
Richelieu could now proceed at leisure to procure
the dissolution of her marriage with Gaston. This
union he had always regarded with such aversion
that contemporaries attributed it to the desire to

marry his niece to the heir of the French throne. At
first it was decided to appeal to the pope for a
divorce, but Urban VIII. insisted upon trying the
case at Rome, and Richelieu dreaded delay and
Spanish influence. Accordingly a civil suit was instituted before the parliament of Paris under the
absurd form of a charge of abduction against the
duke of Lorraine. The decision of the court was
pronounced on September 5, 1634. The marriage
was declared to have been invalidly contracted, and
Charles IV. was found guilty of treason. To appease
the pope an envoy was sent to Rome to explain that
the decision did not affect the ecclesiastical aspect
of the marriage, and that there was no intention to
contest the papal jurisdiction.

About this time Mary de Medici, weary of her
exile in Brussels, and jealous of Puylaurens, who
would allow her no influence over her second son,
made overtures for a reconciliation with the king
and cardinal. But Richelieu would have nothing to
do with his former patroness, and had little difficulty in inducing Louis XIII. to fix impossible conditions as the price of his mother's return. At the
same time he was as anxious as ever for a reconciliation with Gaston, whose return was almost neces-

sary to secure the unity of France in the face of foreign enemies. Negotiations were being carried on with Brussels when the capture of one of the prince's agents revealed the actual conclusion of a treaty with Spain for the invasion of France. This discovery exasperated the cardinal, and he openly declared to the king in council that there were only two means of foiling his brother's intrigues. The one was the birth of a son, which depended upon the grace of God, and the other was the altering of the succession which involved a revolution in the fundamental laws and traditions of France. The dangers of the latter alternative would not have deterred Richelieu from urging its adoption, but it was rendered unnecessary by Gaston's submission. The complete conquest of Lorraine and the active measures which were taken to annul the marriage terrified Gaston and Puylaurens, who had both discovered that the Spaniards only used them as tools for their own ends. A golden bridge was built for the return of the baffled conspirators. Gaston recovered his appanages, with the government of Auvergne instead of Orleans, while Puylaurens, together with the rank of duke and peer, received the hand of a wealthy heiress. But it was soon evident that their acceptance of these terms involved only a partial reconciliation. To the arguments of an ecclesiastical deputation, which tried to convince him of the nullity of his marriage, Gaston lent a polite but evasive attention. It was discovered that he had written to Rome to protest beforehand against the validity of any acts or admissions that might be extorted from him after his return to France. This obstinancy Richelieu attributed to the continued intrigues of Puylaurens, who had indiscreetly boasted that if anything happened to Louis XIII. he would be first minister under his successor. He had to learn that it was safer to plot in Brussels than in Paris, and that his marriage with a relative of the cardinal was not enough to secure his impunity. In February 1635 he was suddenly seized and imprisoned at Vincennes, where a natural death saved him from the penalties of treason. Deprived of his chief adviser and absorbed in sensual pleasures, Gaston fell for a time into insignificance, and was compelled to accept the divorce from Margaret, which was ultimately pronounced by a synod of Gallican clergy.

All this time the Swedes, in spite of their king's death and the vacillation of the elector of Saxony, had been more than holding their own in Germany, while French influence was steadily extended in the southwest. In 1633 the elector of Cologne had formally put his estates under French protection, and the duke of Wurtemberg, unable to defend Montbéliard against the Spaniards, handed over both town and citadel to a French garrison. In the next year several towns in Elsass also threw their gates open to the French, who thus acquired their first footing in a province which was destined to be Richelieu's chief territorial gift to his country.

The chief cause of these successes, and of the failure of the imperial forces to profit by the death of Gustavus Adolphus, was undoubtedly the conduct of Wallenstein. The great general had resumed his command with the firm intention of securing, not the emperor's interests, but his own. With the religious objects of Ferdinand II. and the Catholic League he was entirely out of sympathy. His object was to make himself a great prince of the empire, and to use his military superiority to impose a general pacification upon the warring sects, so as to prevent Germany from being torn in pieces to serve the selfish ends of foreign princes. For Spain, the close and necessary ally of the emperor, he had the greatest hatred. When the Cardinal Infant, Philip IV.'s brother, applied to him for 4000 cavalry, who were needed to bring his army from Milan to Germany, he refused. Instead of vigorously prosecuting the war, he contented himself with his conquest of Bohemia, where he maintained almost royal state, and whence he carried on simultaneous negotiations with Sweden, France, and the Protestant princes of Germany. Richelieu was willing enough to profit by Wallenstein's inactivity, but he had the keenness to detect that antipathy to foreign interference which was at the bottom of his schemes, and he paid little attention to overtures which could bring no advantage to France. But at Vienna it did not need much exercise of Spanish influence to convince Ferdinand that a general who presumed to treat with foreign states as an independent prince could not be tolerated in the imperial service. In his contract with his employer, Wallenstein had been careful to provide against a second dismissal, but he could not secure himself against assassination. As long as his army was faithful he was safe. But the fidelity of his officers was tampered with by Spanish gold, and on February 15, 1634, he fell under the dagger of traitors who received his pay.

The death of Wallenstein marks a great turning-point in the history of the Thirty Years' War. His army was induced to accept the command of the young king of Hungary, Ferdinand's eldest son. In June the Cardinal Infant led his long-delayed expedition into Germany, and his troops succeeded in joining those of the emperor. At Nordlingen the united armies inflicted a crushing defeat upon the Swedes under Horn and Bernard of Saxe-Weimar. For the moment it seemed as if the work of Gustavus Adolphus would be undone by the first failure of his successors. The League of Heilbronn, the product of the joint diplomacy of Richelieu and Oxenstiern, was broken to pieces. John George of Saxony hastened to accept the treaty of Prague (May 1635), by which the Edict of Restitution was revoked, and a compromise was arranged between Catholics and Lutherans. Within a few months these terms were accepted by all the Lutheran princes. As far as Germany was concerned, the Thirty Years' War was at an end. The great questions at issue at its commencement had received a solution which satisfied everybody except the German Calvinists, and they were too few and too powerless to continue hostilities by themselves. But the war had long ceased to be a purely German struggle. In the course of years the German contest had come to involve in itself all the rivalries and enmities which agitated Europe: the quarrels of Sweden and Poland, the jealousy of Denmark against its northern neighbour, the struggle of Spain to reduce the Dutch into subjection, and, above all, the enmity between France and Spain, which dated back to the time of Charles V. It was these foreign interests that prolonged the war for the next thirteen years.

The great schemes of Richelieu would have been ruined if the war had been ended by the treaty of Prague. It is true that the battle of Nordlingen, by weakening Sweden, had brought some direct gains to France. The Swedes, who had seized Philipsburg from the Spaniards, and had hitherto evaded the French demands for its surrender, were compelled to abandon the fortress, and Colmar and other strong places in Elsass endeavoured to obtain security by the admission of French garrisons. But these and the earlier acquisitions would have to be surrendered at a general pacification, and Richelieu had no intention of surrendering them. Nor was this the only danger. The termination of the German war would enormously strengthen Spain. If the Spaniards, freed from the heavy obligation of supporting Austria, could reduce the Dutch or make peace with them, they would then be able to throw all their might into the recovery of their omnipotence in Italy, or even into a direct attack upon France. And France would be left without an efficient ally, as Sweden could render little service in a struggle with Spain.

To avoid these certain and possible disasters, it was necessary that the war should be continued; and to secure its continuation only one expedient remained—the open intervention of France. For such a step Richelieu had long been preparing, and it would have been easy enough to find a pretext for hostilities, even if Spain had not gone out of her way to provide one. In March 1635 a Spanish force sallied from Luxemburg, surprised the city of Trier, and carried off the elector a prisoner to the Netherlands. Richelieu at once sent to the Cardinal Infant to demand the release of an ecclesiastical dignitary whose sole offence was his alliance with France. A refusal was followed by the appearance of a French herald in Brussels, who, with all the old formalities, declared war against the king of Spain. Richelieu had engaged France in the greatest European struggle in which that country had taken part since the death of Henry II.

CHAPTER VII

REVERSES AND TRIUMPHS
1635–1640

RICHELIEU had long contemplated the possibility
of France being forced to take direct part in the
war, and he had made ample preparations, so far
as they could be effected by diplomacy. He had
failed, it is true, to maintain the alliance between
Sweden and the Lutheran princes of Germany, and
he had never been able to detach the members of
the Catholic League from their union with the emperor. On the other hand, he had arranged an offen-
sive and defensive alliance with the United
Provinces, by which the combined forces of the
two states were to be placed under the command
of Frederick Henry, the stadtholder. He had hopes
of a rising in the Netherlands, where many of the
nobles were discontented with the direct rule of
Spain, which had been re-established on the death

of the Infanta. The neutrality of England was assured by Charles I.'s resolution to dispense with a parliament, without which he could not hope to obtain the supplies for a war. With Oxenstiern, who visited Paris in person for the purpose, a treaty was concluded by which France and Sweden pledged themselves to conclude no separate peace with either Austria or Spain. Richelieu's aptest pupil in diplomacy, the count d'Avaux, had foiled the confident attempt of Austria to hamper Sweden by reviving the old feelings of jealousy on the part of Poland and Denmark. The truce between Sweden and Poland, originally concluded by French mediation, was prolonged for another twenty-five years by the same agency. In Italy, Richelieu arranged a league with Savoy, Parma, and Mantua for the partition of the duchy of Milan, and he had hopes that Urban VIII., always jealous of Spanish domination, might be brought to regard the scheme without disfavour. Finally, the duke de Rohan, who had been skilfully converted from a dangerous opponent into a loyal agent, was despatched, with the approval of the Grisons, to occupy the Valtelline, and thus to prevent assistance being sent from Germany to the Milanese. If these grand schemes

had all been attended with success, the power of
Spain beyond the limits of the peninsula would
have been almost annihilated.

But the most active and far-seeing diplomacy
could create neither a trained and disciplined army,
nor competent generals in a country which for the
last generation had been engaged in nothing but
short outbursts of civil war, varied by an occasional
brief expedition to Italy. The numbers of the
French forces, amounting in all to 130,000 men,
excited the astonishment of Europe, where no equal
effort had been made during sixteen years of incessant warfare. But nothing was gained to correspond
to these exhausting preparations. The campaign in
the Netherlands, to which Richelieu attached the
greatest importance, ended in complete failure.
The expected rising never took place, as discontent
with Spanish rule gave way to patriotic indignation at the outrages of French invaders. The arrival of imperial troops, set free by the treaty of
Prague, enabled the Spaniards to raise the siege of
Louvain, and Frederick Henry of Orange, who
commanded the combined French and Dutch
forces, was not strong or enterprising enough to
risk a battle in the open field. On the German fron-

tiers the French succeeded in defending their position in Elsass and Lorraine, but their aid was not sufficient to enable Bernhard of Saxe-Weimar to hold his own on the Rhine. By the end of 1635 Frankfort, Mannheim, Heidelberg, and Mainz had fallen into the hands of the Imperialists. In Italy, although Rohan succeeded in occupying the Valtelline, and thus cut off German aid from Lombardy, the attempted invasion of the Milanese proved a fiasco. Victor Amadeus and Créqui, at the head of a large force of Piedmontese and French, wasted the whole summer in a futile siege of Valenza. Meanwhile the Spaniards enjoyed a complete ascendency at sea, which enabled them to maintain a constant intercourse both with the Netherlands and the Italian peninsula. It was a bitter humiliation for France when a Spanish fleet occupied and garrisoned the two little islands of Lérins, off the coast of Provence.

Richelieu's magnificent schemes of conquest were for the time at an end, and the cardinal himself is not free from some responsibility for his failure. His past experience had taught him to be always suspicious, and he could not trust his generals. He was so long used to command himself, and so confident in his own capacity, that he thought his orders from a distance must be better than those of a mistrusted subordinate on the spot. When possible, he divided the command, so that differences between the two generals might secure his own supremacy. But the chief cause of failure is to be found in the character of the French soldiery. In the course of three generations of civil strife they had lost every military virtue except courage. They could fight in face of the enemy, but in camp they were disorderly, mutinous, impatient alike of hardship and of control. Against veterans trained in the school of Gustavus and of Tilly such troops were worse than useless. But for the support of Bernhard of Saxe-Weimar and his hardy mercenaries the campaign of 1635 would have been still more disastrous.

In spite of the check he had received, Richelieu determined to continue his aggressive policy in 1636. In Italy Victor Amadeus and Créqui advanced to the Ticino, where they inflicted a crushing defeat on the Spanish army. But the duke of Savoy was on bad terms with his colleague, and prevented any attempt to join Rohan, who was waiting near Lake Como for a combined advance upon

Milan. In August the troops returned to winter quarters. Meanwhile a French army had invaded Franche Comté and laid siege to Dôle. But the population was better treated, and therefore more loyal than that of any other Spanish province, and Dôle was still untaken when the unexpected news arrived that France itself was exposed to a formidable invasion. Frederick Henry had succeeded in retaking the fortress of Schenk, which the enemy had captured in the previous year, and the French troops in the Netherlands were preparing to relieve Liége, besieged by the imperial general Piccolomini. But the arrival of the Bavarian commander, John of Werth, and of a considerable Spanish force, under the Cardinal Infant Leopold, encouraged the enemy to attempt a more ambitious enterprise. Patching up terms with the Liégeois, the imperial troops marched southwards, and in July crossed the frontier of Picardy. No preparations had been made for resistance. The border fortresses of La Chapelle and Le Câtelet surrendered at the first summons, the passage of the Somme was forced with ease, and the enemy advanced burning and ravaging to the banks of the Oise. So great was the terror inspired by his mounted Croats that the

name of John of Werth served French mothers
for years as a bogey to frighten children with.

Paris was panic-stricken. Louis XIII., always
gloomy, was more reserved than ever. Everybody
seemed to throw the responsibility for danger and
disaster upon the minister who had declared war.
Richelieu alone preserved his courage and presence
of mind in a crisis that would have daunted a lesser
man. In spite of the entreaties and warnings of his
friends, he proceeded almost unattended through
the streets to the Hôtel de Ville to call upon the
citizens to make sacrifices for the safety of their
country. The effect of his undaunted resolution
and confidence was magical. Paris hastened to re-
spond to his appeal with a devotion like that which
was shown a century and a half later in the revolu-
tionary wars. The municipality, the parliament,
the Sorbonne, and the trading guilds vied with
each other in offering grants of money, and volunteers hastened to enrol their names on the list which
was drawn up in the Hôtel de Ville. The example
of Paris was followed by the other large towns,
and the Huguenots were as eager to prove their
patriotism as the Catholics. Richelieu had many
enemies, but for the moment men thought only of
his services to the country.

The danger proved less than it had at first appeared. The invaders succeeded in taking Corbie, but they never advanced beyond the Oise. The Dutch were threatening the Netherlands, and the Cardinal Infant feared to involve his troops too far in the interior of France. By the time that the new levies were ready to take the field, John of Werth was in full retreat towards the frontier. No attempt was made to harass the enemy, and the French army contented itself with undertaking the siege of Corbie, which was forced to open its gates in November. At the same time an attempted invasion of Burgundy by the duke of Lorraine was successfully repulsed. France had failed to make conquests, but within its own frontiers it was still invincible.

But though France was saved, the minister was still exposed to personal danger. The Spaniards had striven to revive internal disunion, and the manifesto of the Cardinal Infant had been filled with denunciations of Richelieu. The duke of Orleans and the count of Soissons, instead of being conciliated by their appointments to command the army of defence, thought only of the opportunity to gratify their personal ambition or their desire for vengeance. Soissons had been irritated by the refusal of the command in Elsass, entrusted to the

cardinal de la Valette, and deemed himself insulted
by the proposal of a marriage with Richelieu's
niece, Madame de Combalet. The two princes, laying aside their former animosity, formed a dangerous conspiracy against the object of their mutual
hatred. Their schemes went so far as to project the
assassination of the cardinal at Amiens, but Gaston's courage failed him at the moment when he
should have given the concerted signal. The failure
of the Spanish invasion and the recapture of Corbie discouraged the conspirators, and an attempt
to tamper with the fidelity of the troops proved
futile. Dreading discovery and arrest, the two
princes fled from the army in November, Gaston to
Blois and Soissons to Sedan. Negotiations proving
futile, the king and cardinal led an army against
Blois in January 1637. Gaston was unprepared for
resistance, and was allowed to make peace on easy
terms. Soissons, more obstinate or more distrustful,
held out till July, when he also made his submission,
but refused to return to court.

Unfortunately discontent was by no means confined to the princes and great nobles. The middle
and lower classes resented the heavy taxation which
was rendered necessary by the war. Brilliant suc-

cesses might have kindled a spirit of patriotic self-sacrifice, but these successes were still to be won. The parliaments made themselves the organs of local dissatisfaction. In Normandy the opposition of Rouen to the financial edicts of 1637 was only overcome by a threatened advance of king and cardinal at the head of an army. In Guienne citizens and peasants rose in armed revolt against the tax-collectors. But the monarchy, as usual, profited by class divisions. The duke of la Valette, one of Richelieu's most active opponents, took command of the royal troops and put down the rebels. To suppress local independence Richelieu extended the use of intendants in 1637, and thus forged the most powerful link in the chain which bound France in servitude to an absolute monarchy.

While the cardinal was engaged in defeating open opposition, his power was threatened by an extraordinary court intrigue, in which religion and love were curiously intermingled. Louis XIII., though constitutionally chaste, had all a Bourbon's delight in feminine society. Alienated from his wife by political and personal antipathy, he was accustomed to cherish a platonic attachment for one of the ladies of his court. For some years his virtuous

affection had been fixed upon Mademoiselle de
Hautefort, the recognised beauty of Parisian society. But the titular mistress was a devoted admirer of the neglected Anne of Austria, and used
all her influence to inspire the king with distrust
of the cardinal, whom she regarded as the chief
barrier between the royal husband and wife. Richelieu and his supporters were delighted when, in
1635, Louis transferred his affections to Louise de
la Fayette, a beautiful and pensive brunette, whose
personal attractions were equalled by her piety. The
new favourite was a relative of Father Joseph, and
the king's devotion seemed likely to strengthen the
cardinal's ascendency. But Richelieu's energetic
and almost ruthless policy had little fascination for
women, and the innocent Mademoiselle de la Fayette became the tool of a hostile cabal. Its leader
was a Jesuit, Père Caussin, the royal confessor, who
shared the general distrust of his order towards the
cardinal. But the growing affection of the king
excited the scruples of the maid-of-honour, and
she wished to escape danger by entering the clois-
ter. This pious resolution was applauded and encouraged by Richelieu and his supporters. On the
other hand, her relatives and the zealous Caussin

strove to persuade her that she could remain at court without risk to her virtue. Few more curious incidents are recorded in French history than this struggle to repress or to aid the monastic inclinations of a young girl. At last, whether frightened by royal tenderness, or won over by the advice of the Dominican agents of Richelieu, Mademoiselle de la Fayette entered the convent of the Visitation in the rue St. Antoine (May 19, 1637). But the battle was only half won. The king, who applauded while he deplored the resolution of his mistress, continued to visit her at her convent, and her denunciations of the cardinal were the more vigorous now that her virtue was protected by her vows and the convent bars through which the conversation was conducted. The influence of Père Caussin over the king seemed to be stronger than ever, and an open contest began between the confessor and the minister. But the ties which bound Louis XIII. to the cardinal were too strong to be broken even by the combined weight of priestly and feminine influence. In December 1637 Père Caussin was exiled to Rennes, and the king ceased his visits to the convent of the Visitation.

Meanwhile the war continued to be waged in

1637, as before, with varying success. The death of
Ferdinand II. in February made little difference to
a struggle of which he had been a principal author.
Although the new emperor, Ferdinand III., was
more pacifically disposed than his father, he was
forced to continue hostilities by the refusal of
France and Sweden to recognise an election in
which the archbishop of Trier, still a prisoner, had
taken no part. Richelieu made his great effort in
this year in the Netherlands, whither he sent his
friend, the cardinal de la Valette, to co-operate
with Frederick Henry. But the militant cardinal
did little to justify the confidence of his patron.
His only achievements were the capture of two
places in Flanders, and the recovery of the frontier fortress of La Chapelle, while the Prince of
Orange, more careful of Dutch than of French interests, contented himself with laying siege to
Breda, which surrendered in October. These slight
successes were more than counterbalanced by losses
in Germany and in Italy. In Germany the Imperialists carried all before them. The Swedes were driven
from Pomerania, John of Werth took Ehrenbreitstein and Hanau, while Bernhard of Saxe-Weimar,
who had overrun Franche Comté, failed in his

attempt to relieve the last fortress, so that the French lost their last hold on the coveted province of Elsass. In Italy the successive deaths of the dukes of Savoy and Mantua broke up the coalition which Richelieu had formed against the Hapsburgs, and the duke of Parma was forced by the invasion of his duchy to desert the French alliance. Still more serious was the expulsion of Rohan from the Grisons, and the recovery of the Valtelline by Spain. For once, sacrificing religious to political considerations, the Spaniards offered the Protestants greater concessions than even France had been willing to give. The Grisons accepted the bribe, and undertook to rise against the French, whom they had welcomed as deliverers. Rohan found his position untenable without native support, and was forced to evacuate the territory of the Leagues. The Hapsburgs thus recovered the interrupted communications between Tyrol and Lombardy. The only counterpoise to these disasters was an event which must have been peculiarly gratifying to Richelieu. For ten years he had laboured to create a French navy, and in 1636 he had been rewarded by the appearance in the Mediterranean of a fleet of more than forty vessels. Nothing was achieved in that year, owing to want of agreement between the joint commanders, count Harcourt and the archbishop of Bordeaux. But in 1637 the fleet sailed from the harbours of Provence, and after threatening a descent upon Sardinia, returned to recover the two islands of Lérins, which had been occupied for two years by the Spaniards. It was a small triumph in itself, but it was a relief to the national pride, and it presaged a great change in the balance of maritime power in Southern Europe. A powerful French navy could inflict more damage upon the scattered empire of Spain than a succession of the most brilliant victories by land.

The Thirty Years' War had developed, mainly under Richelieu's guidance, into a duel between the houses of Hapsburg and Bourbon, and it was evident that the struggle would be long and desperate. But Richelieu showed no signs of flinching from the task which he had undertaken. He was resolute not to make peace until he had obtained substantial advantages for his country, and until he had broken the power of her rival. France, in spite of financial mismanagement, was the least exhausted of the combatants. The campaign of 1637, although it had not been dazzlingly successful, had at any rate opened the prospect of better things. It was with some confidence that the cardinal set to work to renew his alliance with the Swedes and Bernhard of Saxe-Weimar, while he made strenuous preparations for simultaneous hostilities in Elsass, the Netherlands, Italy, the Spanish frontier, and on the sea. Of so many enterprises, it was impossible that all should be equally successful, but it may be safely affirmed that none was without important and lasting results.

With the year 1638 begins the series of triumphs which have given to Richelieu his almost unequalled reputation as a statesman. If he had died at the end of 1637 he would be remembered as a great home minister, who had crushed the princes, rendered the Huguenots powerless, and supplied the despotic monarchy with an efficient administrative machinery. It was during the next five years that he earned undying fame as the man who crushed the power of the house of Hapsburg, secured the ascendency of the house of Bourbon, and gave an impulse to the history of Europe which was felt for more than a century after his death. And he has the further claim to admiration that for all his achievements both at home and abroad he had

consciously and intentionally laboured. Hitherto
we have been tracing the period of preparation and
of partial failure. Space allows only a brief effort to
point out the direction and extent of his triumphs.

The first, and perhaps in French eyes the greatest
of Richelieu's successes was the conquest of Elsass.
The hero of this achievement was Bernhard of
Saxe Weimar, a descendant of the Albertine line of
Saxony, which had championed the Protestant
cause against Charles V., and had paid for its religious zeal by the confiscation of its territories.
Bernhard's great ambition was to revive the glories
of his family by the acquisition of a German principality. It was with this object that he had joined
the Swedes, and after the death of Gustavus Adolphus he had almost succeeded in erecting a principality in Franconia. But the battle of Nordlingen
had destroyed his hopes, and had forced him to accept the French alliance as the only means of making head against the emperor. Richelieu had hastened to secure so valuable an ally by promising
him French aid in acquiring the landgraviate of
Elsass, the oldest possession of the Austrian Hapsburgs. For three years, owing mainly to the absorption of France in the Netherlands, Bernhard had

made little advance towards the goal of his endeavours. But in 1638 Richelieu decided to make Elsass the principal scene of warfare. He paid up the arrears of the promised subsidies, and promised to make no treaty which did not secure the interests of Bernhard and his army. Thus encouraged, Bernhard hastened to take the field before the winter was over. He had already captured three towns in the Breisgau, and was besieging Rheinfelden when the Imperialists attacked his camp, and after an obstinate struggle forced him to retreat. Nothing daunted by this check, he reorganised his forces, and three days later fell upon the enemy while they were still celebrating their victory. The surprise was completely successful. The Imperialist generals, among whom was the famous John of Werth, fell, with the standards and artillery, into Bernhard's hands. Rheinfelden at once surrendered, and in a few weeks the whole of the Breisgau was reduced to submission.

Bernhard now crossed to the right bank of the Rhine and laid siege to Breisach, the famous fortress which commanded Elsass, and enabled its possessor to control the line of communication between Italy and the Netherlands. The importance of Breisach

was fully realised by the Spaniards, and number-
less efforts were made to relieve the garrison. But
Bernhard succeeded in repulsing all attacks, and
on December 19 Breisach was forced to open its
gates. The conquest of Elsass was assured. But the
advantage to France was by no means so immediate
or obvious. Bernhard was fighting his own battle
and that of Protestantism, and had no intention of
being used as a catspaw by his ally. To the demand
that he should recognise French suzerainty over
Elsass, he replied that he would not be the first to
partition the German Empire. But the erection of
an independent and powerful principality on the
French frontier was by no means in accordance
with Richelieu's wishes. Bernhard seemed likely to
prove as inconvenient and unmanageable as Gustavus Adolphus. But here fortune came to the assistance of France, as it had done in 1632. Bernhard was eager to secure his new principality by
forcing the emperor to make peace. To effect this
he determined in 1639 to march westward in order
to support the Swedish general, Baner, who was
invading Bohemia. But his health was already
broken by anxieties and fatigue, and he had hardly
crossed the Rhine when he died, on July 15, at the

age of thirty-six. By his will he left his army to the joint command of his generals, and his territories to whichever of his brothers would accept them. Bernhard's death was Richelieu's opportunity. French gold purchased the allegiance of the German officers and troops, who accepted a French commander and admitted a French garrison into Breisach. France had secured a hold upon Elsass which nothing but a series of signal and unexpected reverses could compel her to relax. At the same time a fatal blow was dealt at the cohesion of the Spanish Empire.

In Italy the French triumphs, though rather later, were hardly less decisive, and they were the more gratifying because they were directly due to the courage and generalship of Frenchmen. The death of Victor Amadeus of Savoy had left the regency for his infant son in the hands of his widow, Christine. She was a sister of Louis XIII., but she was anxious to adopt a neutral attitude in order to secure the interests of her children. She was, however, forced into a French alliance by the diplomacy of Richelieu, and by the open hostility of the Spaniards, who found allies in her brothers-in-law, Thomas and Maurice. Armed with an im-

perial edict annulling the will of the late duke, and
supported by Lleganes, the Spanish governor of
Milan, the two princes headed a revolt in Piedmont
against Christine. Richelieu did not hesitate to take
advantage of the duchess's difficulties to secure the
interests of France, and demanded the admission of
French garrisons into the capital and chief fortresses of Piedmont. But Christine, whose public
conduct was more creditable than her private life,
refused to sacrifice the independence of her son's
territories even to her own brother. She would only
consent to the temporary occupation of three
minor fortresses. For the moment she suffered for
her patriotism: in the autumn of 1639 both Turin
and Nice fell into the hands of her opponents, and
she was formally deposed from the regency.

Christine now fled from Piedmont to Savoy,
whither she had already sent the young duke for
safety. At Grenoble she had a personal interview
with Louis XIII. and the cardinal, and again discovered that disinterested assistance was the last
thing she could expect from the country of her
birth. Richelieu demanded that the young duke
should be sent to Paris to be educated, and that the
whole of Savoy, together with the places in Pied-

mont which still held out, should be handed over
to French occupation. But the duchess, hard pressed
as she was, refused to entrust her son to foreign
custody, and insisted upon reserving the fortress of
Montmelian as his residence. Richelieu did not con-
ceal his irritation at what he called Christine's
obstinacy, but he could not allow the Spaniards to
retain their hold on Piedmont. The cardinal de la
Valette, who had been sent to command in Italy,
had died there in September 1639. He was the only
son of Epernon, who was loyal to Richelieu, and
he owed his military employments more to the
minister's gratitude than to his own capacity. His
place was taken by Count Harcourt, the first of the
distinguished French generals who obtained their
training in this war. In 1640 Harcourt commenced
the campaign which laid the foundation for the
military prestige of France. By a bold march he
forced Lleganes, though at the head of a vastly superior force, to raise the siege of Casale. Thence the
French returned to undertake the siege of Turin.
Meanwhile Lleganes collected all the Spanish troops
and advanced to the aid of Prince Thomas, who
commanded the defending garrison. Harcourt
found himself at once besieger and besieged, and

his army was threatened with disease and starvation. Fortunately the enemy, instead of harassing the French and avoiding a direct conflict, tried to crush them by a combined attack. After a desperate struggle under the walls of Turin, Harcourt succeeded not only in forcing the garrison back to the city, but also in driving the Spaniards from their position. After two months of blockade the garrison could hold out no longer. A last effort on the part of Lleganes to break through the besiegers was repulsed, and on September 22 Turin opened its gates. "I would rather be Count Harcourt than emperor!" said the captive John of Werth, when he heard the news of this achievement. In November Christine returned to her capital amidst the applause of the citizens. By the end of another year the Spaniards had been completely driven from Piedmont.

For the victories in Italy Richelieu was indebted to the capacity of subordinates, whom he had selected and inspired, but whose actions he could not direct. For the naval triumphs of France he may claim far more personal glory, as he was the virtual creator of the French navy. Hitherto the only achievement of the fleet had been the capture

of the Lérins, and there had been no attempt to
meet the Spaniards in open battle. But the year
1638 witnessed the first serious blow to that maritime ascendency without which Spain could hardly
defend its own territories, much less prove formidable to foreign states. On August 22 Archbishop Sourdis attacked and almost destroyed a
Spanish squadron off Guetaria in the Bay of Biscay.
Only a week later fifteen French vessels under
Pont-Courlay, a nephew of Richelieu, assaulted an
equal number of Spanish ships near Genoa. The
struggle was long and exhausting, but the superior
artillery of the French gave them an advantage at
close quarters, and their victory was crowned by
the capture of the Spanish admiral. This success,
though smaller, was even more significant than that
of Guetaria, because the Spanish power had, since
Lepanto, no rival on the Mediterranean, whereas
in the northern seas it was already threatened by
the growing navy of the United Provinces. In 1639
events at sea were still more decisive. A large
Spanish fleet succeeded in evading the watchfulness
of Sourdis, and reached the English Channel. There
it met the Dutch under Martin Tromp, and after
fighting for two days the Spaniards sought the

Downs and the shelter of the English coast. While Charles I. was higgling with Spain about the price to be paid for his protection, Richelieu succeeded in conveying to Tromp an intimation to disregard the threats of England. Nothing loth, the Dutch admiral sailed against the Spanish fleet, and almost completely destroyed it (October 11). Barely ten of the great galleons succeeded in reaching Dunkirk in safety. Spain had experienced no such crushing disaster since the loss of the great Armada. With its fleet shattered and Breisach in the hands of the French, it was almost impossible to send assistance to the Netherlands.

Since the treaty of 1629 Richelieu had little to fear from the hostility of England. Charles I. seemed determined to maintain an inexpensive if inglorious neutrality, and he was alienated from Spain by the steady refusal to do anything for the Palatine family. But the growing naval power of France excited misgivings in England. Charles was indignant at the insult to the English flag in the Downs, and Henrietta Maria was not disinclined to espouse the cause of her mother against the minister who condemned her to life-long exile. But Richelieu had weapons ready to hand against the

English king, and he did not scruple to use them. French agents and French money had no small part in stirring up that Scotch rebellion which dealt the first fatal blow to Stuart despotism. And when the expenses and failures of the war forced Charles at last to summon the Long Parliament, Richelieu did not hesitate to establish relations with the opposition party, which had less cause than the king to favour Spain. No doubt the Great Rebellion would have arisen if Richelieu had never lived, but he had some share in moulding the actual events which led to it. It was even reported and believed that when Charles endeavoured to seize the five members, the warning which enabled them to escape came from the French ambassador. The minister who did more than any other man to establish absolutism in France may claim to have assisted—from purely selfish motives—in the vindication of liberty in England.

The same keen insight which enabled Richelieu to appreciate and make use of the elements of discontent and opposition in England and Scotland was equally apparent in his relations with the Spanish peninsula. Spain, unlike France, was never a united state. The Hapsburgs were primarily kings

of Castile, and they ruled the other parts of the
peninsula as dependent provinces, no better off
than Naples or Milan. This policy was not likely
to conciliate a population in which local prejudices
and traditions were always stronger than central
interests. The two extremes of the peninsula, Portugal and Catalonia, were especially alienated by a
government which trampled upon their pride and
their aspirations to independence. Olivares, the all-
powerful minister of Philip IV., saw the weakness
of Spain, but could not devise the proper remedy.
He attributed the superiority of France, quite
rightly, to its greater unity and centralisation, and
thought to exalt his own country by imitating the
government of his rival. But it was not easy to make
the bonds more tolerable merely by tightening
them. The only result of his premature experiment
was to provoke a double rebellion, which France
was quite ready to ferment and to use for its own
advantage.

The local militia of Catalonia had loyally defended the little province of Roussillon against
French invasion in 1639. But the people resented
the outrages of the Castilian troops, who were
quartered upon them during the winter. Early in

1640 Olivares issued an edict ordering the enrol-
ment of all men capable of bearing arms to serve
wherever they should be sent. This was contrary to
the traditional privileges of the provinces, and excited a general revolt. As the government of
Madrid would make no concessions, the rebels
turned for assistance to France. Richelieu had no
scruples about the legitimacy of a revolt which
served his plans, and promised to send officers and
8000 men to aid the Catalans. Nor was a mere diversion of the enemy's attention the only result at
which he aimed. In January 1641 a treaty was
arranged by which the Catalans were to become
not only the allies but the subjects of France, on
condition that their liberties should be respected.
The Pyrenees had never been a boundary, and for
centuries Spanish rule had extended north of the
mountain range. Now France threatened to advance to the Ebro, once the limit of the power of
Charles the Great.

The example of Catalonia was promptly followed by Portugal, which had been annexed by
Philip II. in 1580, but had never acquiesced in the
rule of its conquerors. From the first declaration
of war Richelieu had reckoned upon Portuguese

assistance, and his agents had been busy in encouraging and stirring up discontent. Probably the revolt would have begun sooner but for the moderation or timidity of the duke of Braganza, the largest landholder in Portugal and the representative of the old royal line. But in 1640 circumstances were too favourable to be neglected. The nobles refused to obey the order of Olivares to march against Catalonia, and could only avoid the penalty of disobedience by rebellion. The scruples of the duke of Braganza were overcome by French representations, and in December he was proclaimed king as John IV. Never was a revolution accomplished with greater ease or unanimity. The first act of the new king was to conclude a treaty with France, which promised to aid him against Spain, while he pledged himself to conclude no treaty without French approval.

In the Netherlands events were not so rapid or decisive as elsewhere; but here also the year 1640 witnessed an important triumph for France. In June the French army laid siege to Arras, the strongly-fortified capital of the border province of Artois. Artois was an ancient fief of France, but had been freed from vassalage by Charles V. The

Cardinal Infant and the duke of Lorraine tried to harass the besiegers by occupying the adjacent country and cutting off supplies. Richelieu himself went to Amiens to superintend the sending of reinforcements and provisions to Arras. A regular army was formed to conduct the convoy. Before it could arrive the Spaniards made a desperate attack upon the French camp, but were repulsed. This failure was decisive. On August 9 the town of Arras was surrendered, and the province of Artois was declared to be reunited to the French crown. It was a conquest which France was not likely to relinquish.

The aspect of affairs had undergone a startling change since 1636. In that year the Spaniards had been victors on French soil, and their advance had excited a panic in the French capital. In 1640 France was not only secure against invasion, but its frontier had been advanced in the east, in the north, and in the south, and its great rival, Spain, was threatened with imminent dissolution. The connection with the Netherlands was already destroyed, and the French fleet in the Mediterranean made communication with Italy difficult and dangerous. In the peninsula itself two provinces were in open revolt, and one of them seemed likely to become a part of France. The man who, in five years, had produced such marvellous results was Richelieu.

While the cardinal's foreign policy had been attended with such gratifying success, an event had occurred at home which he regarded with even greater satisfaction. The essential weakness of Richelieu's position was the fact that Louis XIII. was childless, and that the heir to the throne was his inveterate opponent, the feeble and vicious Gaston of Orleans. But on September 5, 1638, after twenty-three years of married life, Anne of Austria rendered her first service to the minister whom she detested by giving birth to a dauphin, afterwards Louis XIV. Richelieu presented a diamond rose to the messenger who brought him the welcome news, and all France shared in his exultation. In 1640 the succession was still further secured by the birth of a second son, the ancestor of the house of Orleans.

One misfortune clouded the felicity of the grand period of Richelieu's career. In December 1638, just after the news of the capture of Breisach, he lost Father Joseph, "his prop and consolation," as

he called him in the first fervour of his grief.
Richelieu's detractors have not hesitated to make
the most of the obscurity which covers the relations between these two men. They have contended
that Father Joseph was the brain and Richelieu the
arm; that the red cardinal was only the marionette
who danced before the public, while the grey cardinal pulled the strings. To such assertions or in-
nuendoes no answer is possible except that there is
no evidence for it, and against it we have not only
antecedent improbability, but the fact that Richelieu's policy and character show no signs of vacillation or weakness after the death of his friend. The
only reasonable conclusion is that the Capuchin
monk was the most able and perhaps the most
trusted of the few confidential agents whom
Richelieu collected round him, but that there is no
ground for believing that he was more than a familiar adviser whose counsel was always valued,
but not always adopted.

CHAPTER VIII

DOMESTIC GOVERNMENT

THE foremost statesmen of history may be roughly divided into two chief classes. Some are great diplomatists, endowed with a natural gift for understanding and influencing the relations between the great states of their time, and they employ this gift to such purpose as to secure the prestige and the material advancement of their own country, and thereby profoundly influence the general history of the world. Others concentrate their attention mainly upon domestic problems: either upon economic questions, such as the development of trade, or manufactures, or colonisation; or upon more purely political questions, such as the relations of classes to each other or to the crown, the extension or limitation of local independence, the widening or narrowing of the basis of government. It is one of Richelieu's claims to exceptional distinction that he belongs to both these classes. For good or for evil, he left an ineffaceable mark both upon the general history of Europe and upon the internal development of France. It may be contended that he was more successful as a diplomatist than as a ruler of France, that he was too much absorbed in foreign politics to give sufficient attention to the solution of domestic problems; but there can be no doubt that his influence was equally great in both departments of government.

The aims of Richelieu's domestic policy are extremely simple, and they have been described by himself with equal point and clearness in the "brief narration of the great actions of the king," which he drew up towards the close of his ministry. "When your Majesty resolved to admit me to his council and to a share in his confidence, I can say with truth that the Huguenots divided the State with the monarchy, that the nobles behaved as if they were not subjects, and that the chief governors of provinces acted as if they had been independent sovereigns. . . . I then undertook to employ all my energy and all the authority that you were pleased to give me to ruin the Huguenot faction, to humble the pride of the nobles, to reduce all your subjects to their duty, and to exalt your name to its proper position among foreign nations." Hostile critics have contended that the dangers from the Huguenots and the nobles were less than Richelieu would have us believe, but no one has denied that he made it his first object to establish the unity of France, that he conceived a strong monarchy to be the only basis of that unity, and that he set himself resolutely to remove or destroy all obstacles to the direct and efficient exercise of the central power.

Richelieu's treatment of the Huguenots has been already sufficiently described. He deprived them of their exceptional privileges and securities, reduced them to political impotence, but left them in the enjoyment of religious liberty. The result was that many of the nobles, who had espoused the reformed doctrines mainly as a means of recovering independence, returned to orthodoxy in the hope of gaining court favour. An orderly and governing mind could hardly fail to appreciate the value of uniformity of belief and worship as a bulwark of national unity, and there were not wanting advisers to urge upon Richelieu that a little politic pressure might result in the extinction of a sect with which he had scant reason to sympathise. But the cardinal steadily refused to risk the undoing of the work he had accomplished and to revive religious discord by persecution. His complaint against the Huguenots had been that they were Protestants first and Frenchmen afterwards; if they would only consent to be Frenchmen in the first place, and to regard patriotic devotion as their primary duty, he had no desire to alienate them once more from the state by attempting to enforce religious conformity. His moderation was rewarded with complete success. The Huguenots showed their gratitude by becoming in the next generation not only the most industrious and thrifty, but also the most loyal subjects of the crown. The list of great commanders whose ability turned the scale in the struggle between France and Spain would be sadly diminished, both in numbers and in brilliance, if it had not included such famous Huguenots as Gassion, de la Force, de Rohan, Duquesne, and Turenne.

The Vicomte d'Avenel, in his great work on *Richelieu et la Monarchie Absolue*, has endeavoured to defend the French nobles from the charges of

factious disloyalty which constitute the sole justification of Richelieu's harsh treatment of their
order. But his special pleading, learned and ingeni-
ous as it is, breaks down before the bare facts of
history during the religious wars, the regency of
Mary de Medici, and the Fronde. It is impossible
for any unprejudiced reader of those periods to
avoid the conclusion that as a class the nobles were
the most dangerous and useless part of the population. Their pretensions to lawless independence
were equally inconsistent with the efficiency of the
central government and with the prosperity of
the people. They had ceased to perform most of the
duties which had devolved upon them in the days
of the feudal system, yet they retained all the
privileges and exemptions which they had gained
in consideration of their discharge of these duties.
The relations of the chief nobles with Gaston of
Orleans and the queen-mother, together with the
fact that the foreign enemies of France openly encouraged and exulted in these divisions, would have
justified Richelieu's attitude on the simple ground
of self-defence, even if it were impossible to find
any higher motive for his actions.

The power of the French nobles rested mainly

upon a triple basis: (1) their strongly-fortified castles, each of which required a separate siege for its reduction; (2) their contempt for ordinary jurisdiction, and their claim to settle their own disputes by what had once been their recognised right —private war; (3) the power which they exercised in the provinces through their position as governors. With that insight which is always the highest proof of statesmanship, Richelieu struck directly at the foundations, confident that if they could be overthrown the superstructure would topple down of its own accord. In 1626 two important edicts were issued. One ordered the destruction of all fortresses, except such as were needed for the defence of the frontiers, and forbade in the future the fortification of private houses. The other prohibited duelling on pain of death. The first of these edicts was carried out amidst the applause of burghers and peasants. It has been urged that the compulsory demolition was unnecessary, and therefore of slight importance, that the changed habits of the nobles required comfort rather than fortifications, and that the later style of baronial residence would have come in of its own accord without any action on the part of the government. But this argument

carries with it its own refutation. The changed
habits of the nobles were the result, not the cause,
of their political impotence; and that impotence
arose from the disappearance of the old sense of
impunity, to which the loss of defensible walls un-
questionably contributed. The edict against duels,
in spite of the severity dealt out to Bouteville and
des Chapelles, was not enforced with anything like
the same stringency. Richelieu himself had too
much of the sentiment of his noble birth and his
military training not to feel a real sympathy for the
traditional method of defending personal honour.
No execution for which he was responsible cost him
more hesitation and misgivings than that of Bouteville, and he devotes several pages of his *Memoirs*
to a regretful estimate of his merits and misfortunes. It was rather the general character of Richelieu's administration than the letter of any particular edict which caused the gradual decline of the
practice of duelling.

When Richelieu entered the ministry in 1624 he
found the chief provinces divided among nineteen
governors, all of them belonging to the highest rank
of nobility. These regarded their posts as private
and heritable property to be administered for their

personal interests. Whenever they had occasion to quarrel with the court, it was to their province that they retreated, either as a secure asylum or as a source of strength for attack. By the time of the cardinal's death, only four of these nineteen governors retained their position. The rest had been removed to make room for officials whom the minister could trust. And a terrible lesson of the duty and necessity of obedience had been taught to these local rulers by the defeat and execution of Montmorency in his own province of Languedoc. But by far the greatest blow to the authority of the nobles was dealt by the appointment of intendants. A small literature has arisen in recent years on the subject of the origin of these famous officials. An edict of 1635 which had long been regarded as marking the definite creation of intendants has been conclusively proved to have no reference to them. It has been further proved that *maîtres des requêtes* of the royal council had been frequently sent out to the provinces in the sixteenth century with the title of intendant, and with special instructions to supervise and control local administration. But the tradition which regards Richelieu as their real author has still a substantial foundation.

It was he who made the intendants permanent officials, who extended them to the whole kingdom, and gave them their complete functions as intendants of justice, police, and finance. No single edict determined their appointment or defined their powers, but gradually they obtained the supreme control of all departments of administration, and became the recognised channel of communication between their districts and the royal council. The jealousy which they inspired among the privileged classes is illustrated by the fact that one of the first demands of the Fronde was for their suppression. But under Louis XIV. they were restored, to become the agents of that efficient, if excessive centralisation, which constituted at once the strength and the weakness of the later Bourbon monarchy. The nobles retained their dignity and their revenues as provincial governors, but all substantial authority passed to the middle-class officials, who had neither the means nor the temptation to resist the crown.

It would take too long to examine in detail all the measures taken by Richelieu to simplify and centralise the government of France. He suppressed the ancient and dignified offices of constable and admiral because they gave their holders a power too great to be safely entrusted to a subject. He never summoned the States-General, and he sternly checked the political pretensions of that most interesting and unique of judicial courts, the Parliament of Paris. By an edict of 1641 the parliament was forbidden to take any cognisances of affairs of state, unless its advice was specially asked by the king; all edicts on matters of government or administration are to be registered at once without opposition or debate; on financial matters the parliament is forbidden to introduce amendments; any remonstrances it may wish to make must be presented at once, and if they are rejected, registration is to follow as a matter of course; finally, the old formula of refusal, "we ought not and cannot," is expressly prohibited as injurious to the authority of the prince. Nor was Richelieu content with this suppression of political powers, to which the claim was of more than doubtful validity; he also encroached upon the undoubted rights of jurisdiction which the court had always possessed. In spite of the vigorous and well-justified protests, both of the parliament and of the accused, the trial of prominent political offenders was in all cases withdrawn from the cognisance of the supreme law court, and entrusted to extraordinary commissions nominated for each case. This exceptional jurisdiction, which enabled Richelieu to give a dangerous latitude and vagueness to offenses against the state, was one of the most arbitrary and least defensible features of his administration.

Of the local liberties which had survived in some parts of France Richelieu showed himself the bitter enemy. Most of the provinces were *pays d'élection, i.e.* they were divided into districts in which the assessment and collection of taxes were vested in royal officials called *élus*. But several provinces had retained representative institutions, either by custom or by special agreement made at the time of their annexation to the crown. The chief of these *pays d'états* were Languedoc, Normandy, Brittany, Burgundy, Provence, and Dauphiné. The composition and powers of the provincial estates varied in innumerable details, but all had one common privilege: they made their own financial bargains with the crown, and they appointed their own officials to assess and collect their contributions to the state. The suppression in 1629 of the Huguenot revolt in Languedoc gave Richelieu an opportunity for attempting the suppression of this privilege, and edicts were issued to extend the division into *élections* to all the provinces of France. These edicts were finally enforced in Normandy and Dauphiné. In the latter the estates were altogether abolished, and in Normandy, though the estates continued to meet till their final suppression in 1666, they lost all practical power. In the other provinces the edicts provoked strenuous remonstrances and resistance, to which Richelieu, warned by Montmorency's rising in Languedoc, found it advisable to yield. In Languedoc, Burgundy, and Provence the *élections* were abolished, but these provinces had to purchase the concession by heavy money payments and by accepting conditions which deprived the provincial estates of much of their independence. For instance, in Languedoc, by far the most important of the *pays d'états*, the estates were only allowed to meet every other year; their session was limited to fifteen days, and they were strictly forbidden to levy any tax or loan without the royal approval. In Brittany alone, where the composition of the estates was least democratic, and where Richelieu had special authority, both as governor and as

head of the maritime administration, no special attempt was made to harass the provincial assembly,
which indeed had shown a desire to aid rather than
to impede the minister's policy. But even in Brittany some changes were made to the advantage of
the crown. The nobles lost the right of personal attendance, and could only appear when authorised
by royal letters-patent, and the towns which were
to send deputies to the meeting were to be selected
on each occasion by the governor. In this connection, too, it must be remembered that the institution of intendants contributed to strengthen the
control of the central government over both *pays
d'états* and *pays d'élections.*

One obvious result of Richelieu's policy was to
throw a vast increase of work upon the royal council, and it was necessary to improve its organisation so as to enable it to meet its enlarged duties and
responsibilities. Richelieu's arrangements, which
lasted, with slight changes in detail, till the fall of
the monarchy, may be instructively compared with
the organisation of the Privy Council undertaken
by the Tudor kings under the pressure of similar
necessities. To render the conduct of business regular and uniform the council was split into sections,

which met on special days for the consideration of
particular departments. On Tuesdays was held the
conseil des dépêches, which was responsible for the
provincial administration. To it were sent all re-
ports from the governors and other local officers,
and its functions resemble those of our Home Office. The *conseil des finances* sat twice a week—on
Wednesdays, to consider all questions connected
with assessment and expenditure, and on Thurs-
days, to hear all appeals on financial matters, either
from officials or from private individuals. On Sat-
urdays was held the *conseil des parties* or the *conseil
privé.* This was a purely judicial body. Before it
were brought appeals from other courts to the
crown, and a number of cases of first instance, especially those in which officials were interested,
which were evoked from the ordinary courts to the
royal council. These councils must not be regarded
as distinct bodies, but as parts of the same body.
The great officers of state, the chancellor, the *surintendant des finances,* and the four secretaries of
state, were members of all the divisions, and so were
many of the ordinary councillors. The business of
each section was prepared and reported upon by
a number of *maîtres des requêtes,* who took it in

turns to serve at the council for three months at a
time. At other times they were employed in special
commissions in the royal service. These men formed
the nursery of French administrators, and it was
from among them that the intendants were always
selected.

But this elaborate organisation was only concerned with the routine work of administration.
The *conseil du roy*, like the English Privy Council
under the later Stuarts, had become too numerous
and clumsy a body to provide that secrecy and
concentration which a despotism always requires,
and especially for foreign affairs. The same motives
which led in England to the growth of the Cabinet,
produced a similar institution in France, which
is variously known as the *conseil d'état*, the *conseil
d'en haut, conseil étroit* or *conseil privé*.

It is impossible to describe Richelieu as the founder of this institution, which grew out of obvious
necessities; but it was he who gave it the form and
the importance which it retained till the Revolution. The council of state—to choose one out of its
numerous appellations—had the sole consideration
of foreign affairs, which had formerly gone to the
conseil des dépêches, and it possessed the real initia-

tive and decisive voice in all domestic matters. Its members, who were always nominated by the king, were called *ministres d'état.* The chief officers of state were usually, but not necessarily, included in the council, but the king often admitted men who held no special office. The king himself presided, and in his absence the first minister. The powers of the council were in appearance very great. It quashed the decisions of ordinary courts, it evoked cases for its own consideration, and appointed extraordinary judicial commissions. It issued the edicts which became law on registration by the parliament. It could make peace or war, determine the amount and method of taxation, and supervise the conduct of all other administrative bodies. But these enormous powers were in reality not the powers of the council but of the crown. The ministers of state had no other function than to advise. There was no voting, and no decision by a majority. The members stated their opinion, often in the form of a written memoir, but the king decided at his own pleasure.

Thus Richelieu had erected an administrative system which survived the attacks of nobles and parliament in the Fronde, and justified the boast attributed to Louis XIV., *l'Etat c'est moi!* It is usual, though of doubtful fairness, to hold the cardinal responsible for the fact that succeeding kings abused the powers bequeathed to them, or at any rate failed to use them for the best advantage of their country. It is the inherent vice of despotism that no human ingenuity can provide a succession of men wise and virtuous enough to be intrusted with that omnipotence which in the hands of a perfect ruler may be for a moment the best form of government in the world. Englishmen have, except for a short interval, preferred a government in which there is more balance of forces, more complicated machinery, and less individual initiative and responsibility. Such a system has many unquestionable defects; it is less simple, less logical, and less easy to work than a centralised despotism; but it has the supreme merit of being safer, of leaving less to chance, of resting upon the average capacity of the many, rather than upon the possibility of exceptional capacity in one. Those critics who condemn Richelieu for the ultimate failure of French despotism are of opinion that he ought to have founded, or tried to found, a constitutional government in France like that which gradually grew

up in England. Instead of doing "everything for
the people, and nothing by the people," he should
have allowed the subjects some voice in their own
government. To this criticism there is one simple
and overwhelming answer: it was quite impossible.
It would require a long analysis of French history
and French institutions to furnish conclusive proof
of this assertion, but it can be so established beyond
question. Ever since the thirteenth century there
had been an incurable twist against constitutional-
ism. The secret of the successful beginning of parliamentary government in England is to be found
in the alliance of classes against the crown, which
begins with the great struggle to extort the charter
from John. Such an alliance is conspicuously ab-
sent in France, where from the thirteenth to the
eighteenth century there is no single instance of a
league between the nobles and the third estate to
secure an interest common to both. The jealous hostility of classes in France enabled the crown to play
off one against the other, and thus to raise itself to
unchallenged supremacy. Geographical needs and
the long struggles, first with England and afterwards with Spain, all contributed to the triumph
of the monarchy. No statesman, however great,

can free himself from the influence of historical development, nor can he work with other instruments than those which are supplied to him from the past. In France there were two institutions which at one time or another claimed what we should call constitutional powers. The States-General, after a brief triumph in the middle of the fourteenth century, proved a complete and hopeless failure. The division into three orders, each more zealous for its selfish interests than for the general welfare, and the inability of the third estate to make its influence felt against the ascendency of nobles and clergy, condemned this assembly to sterile impotence. Richelieu himself, as has been seen, was a prominent member of the States-General of 1614, and had seen enough to convince him that the success of France was not to be sought there. No similar assembly met till the eve of the Revolution. The disappearance of the States-General gave increased prominence and importance to the Parliament of Paris, which endeavoured to fill the gap thus created. This hereditary corporation of judges aspired to emulate the English legislature, with which it had nothing in common but the name. The practice of registration enabled them to

claim a right first of remonstrance and afterwards
of veto on all legislation, and their independence
of royal nomination or dismissal gave this claim
an importance which it would not otherwise have
possessed. But it would be the grossest mistake to
argue from the spirited and often just opposition
of the Parliament to despotism that its members
had any sympathy with popular wishes, or any understanding of popular needs. The Parliament of
Paris, as was conclusively shown on the eve of the
Revolution, was really the last and firmest stronghold of official prejudices and class privileges. If
Richelieu ever seriously considered the alternatives
he would have been right in deciding that it was
better to trust the future of France to the monarchy than to a narrow and bigoted bureaucracy.
In the one there was a chance of salvation, in the
other there was none.

The criterion by which Richelieu's government
should be tested is to be sought, not in an estimate
of the successes or blunders of the later Bourbons,
but in an examination as to whether Richelieu himself made the best use of the authority which he
established. That his foreign policy was prudent
and far-sighted, and that it was guided by a single-

minded desire to promote the interests of his
country, has been generally admitted both by
Frenchmen and by foreigners. But it is not easy to
be equally positive about his domestic administration. Many of his measures may doubtless be praised
without reserve. He revived the military organisation, which had fallen into chaos during the disorders of the religious wars. The steps which he
took to increase the numbers of the army by an im-
proved system of recruiting, to develop and systematise the commissariat, and to enforce strict
discipline, anticipated the more thorough reforms
of le Tellier and Louvois, and began the process
which made the French army for half a century
the finest fighting force in the world. Still more
personal credit is due to the naval administration,
to which Richelieu gave strenuous and unflagging
attention. When he came into office there was practically no navy at all, and in time of war the government had to depend upon the vessels it could
hire from individuals. When Sully, under Henry
IV., was sent on an embassy to London, he had to
make the voyage in an English vessel, and we have
seen that Richelieu, in his first measures against
the Huguenots, was forced to employ borrowed

ships from England and Holland. Thus the whole
task of naval construction, of the forming and
training of efficient crews, had to be begun from
the very beginning. But Richelieu's energetic will
was equal to all difficulties. By the time of his death
France possessed thirty-two men of war in the
Mediterranean, and twenty-four on the Atlantic
coast, without counting the smaller vessels. And this
force had shown itself fully capable on more than
one occasion of holding its own against the naval
power of Spain, which had hitherto been without a
rival in Southern Europe. At the same time special
attention was paid to the fortification of naval
ports. The defences of Toulon in the south, and of
Havre in the north, were immensely strengthened.
Richelieu's special interest in Poitou led him to exaggerate the importance of Brouage, on which
large sums of money were wasted; but he more than
redeemed this mistake by creating the port of Brest,
which was destined in the future to be the great
French arsenal on the Atlantic. It is further to his
credit that he recognised the important truth that
the only sound basis of naval power is to be found in a
mercantile marine, and that he spared no pains to
extend French commerce and colonisation. He pro-

tected Mediterranean traders against the pirates of Algiers, Tunis, and Morocco, and he opened fresh markets in the north by commercial treaties with Russia, Sweden, and Denmark. His colonial policy was marred by the practice, common to all statesmen of that day, of entrusting colonial enterprise entirely to exclusive companies. These corporations, by which privileged individuals were protected at the expense of the general body of consumers, were extremely unsuccessful in French hands, partly through their excessive dependence upon state patronage and control and partly through their total neglect of agriculture, and the consequent failure to form permanent and prosperous French settlements. Still, in spite of the inherent defects of the methods he employed, Richelieu's ministry marks a notable era in the history of French colonies. His support secured the restoration to Canada of Quebec and Nova Scotia, which had been seized by the English, and his encouragement also led to the establishment of French settlements on the coast of Guiana and in the West Indian islands of St. Christopher, Martinique, Guadaloupe, and St. Domingo, and in the east to the first attempt to occupy Madagascar.

But against these measures, which were well-intentioned if not always wise, must be set an almost complete neglect of the internal wellbeing of France. In the history of the progress of French agriculture and manufactures there is a distinct and lamentable gap between the time of Sully and that of Colbert. In spite of the strongly-worded protests of the third estate in 1614, Richelieu left production hampered by the system of guilds and privileged corporations, and he made no attempt to remove or limit the provincial customs duties which acted as a barrier to internal trade, and as a hindrance to the complete realisation of national interests and unity. But by far the most serious charge against Richelieu's domestic government is based on his complete failure to reform the abuses of the financial administration of France. The direct taxes, from which the privileged classes were wholly exempt, were extremely oppressive in their incidence, especially in those provinces where the *taille* was levied on personal and not on real property. The indirect taxes, assessed for the most part on the selling prices of commodities, were likewise extremely unequal, and constituted a direct discouragement to exchange. The *gabelle* on

salt was perhaps the most ludicrously iniquitous
tax recorded in the history of any civilised com-
munity. The sale of offices, a practice which had
been going on for more than a century, had given
rise to a disguised national debt, contracted on the
most extravagant and ruinous terms. The practice of farming the indirect taxes, and the constant
insufficiency of the revenue to meet the expenditure, had placed the government at the mercy of
the financiers, who were accustomed to make large
fortunes at the expense of the tax-payers. The secrecy and consequent disorder of the public accounts had facilitated fraud and peculation, and
the reckless concessions to rebellious nobles during
the king's minority had more than undone the reforms which Sully had introduced under Henry IV.

Richelieu was not a trained economist, and many
of the evils of the financial system were doubtless
less obvious in the seventeenth than they are in
the nineteenth century. But that contemporaries
were fully alive to some of the worst abuses, and
were clamorous for their removal, is fully established by the *cahiers* of the third estate in 1614.
That Richelieu himself was equally alive to the
necessity of reform is proved, not so much by the

dubious evidence of the so-called *Testament Politique*, as by numerous passages in his *Memoirs*, and by the detailed proposals which he submitted to the king in 1625. It is equally certain that Richelieu was the only minister in French history who possessed sufficient authority and strength of will to carry through a sweeping measure of financial reform against the interested opposition of the privileged classes, who in the end succeeded in maintaining the old abuses till they were swept away by the Revolution. A few tentative measures were taken in his earlier years, such as the reduction of the *taille* by 600,000 francs, and the appointment of a chamber of justice which mulcted the financiers of some of their ill-gotten gains. But these Acts led to no permanent improvement, and in the meantime the worst evils, the sale of offices, the *gabelle*, and the system of the *ferme*, were left absolutely untouched. And under the growing pressure of military expenditure all idea of reform was ultimately abandoned. Every method of raising the revenue was strained to the uttermost. The opposition of the parliaments, of the provincial estates, and of armed rebellion, as in the case of the famous *Nus-pieds* in Normandy, was ruthlessly suppressed.

New offices were created for the purpose of selling them, and direct loans were raised at an ever-increasing rate of interest. The result was that after Richelieu's death the queen regent found that the revenues of the next three years had been already spent.

It has, of course, been urged by Richelieu's defenders that the greatest and most industrious statesman cannot do everything, and that a period of almost incessant war does not offer a favourable opportunity for the introduction of financial reforms. To the second argument it may be answered that Richelieu was in office for ten years before France was involved in war on a large scale, and that if he had set himself in those ten years to remedy acknowledged abuses, and to abolish or restrict harmful and obsolete privileges, he would have immensely increased the ability of the country to stand the strain of the vastly-increased expenditure after 1635. And to the first argument the possible answer has still more weight. Like many other notable rulers, Richelieu was extremely jealous of the display of any independence or initiative on the part of his colleagues. In choosing them, he did not look for ability or even honesty so much as for absolute submission to himself. The same autocratic assumption that impelled him to control from Paris the operations of generals in the field, led him at home to surround himself, as time went on, with useful tools rather than with men of marked capacity. To this must be attributed the rapid though temporary decline of France after his death. In no branch of administration, except in diplomacy, did Richelieu leave behind him a ready-trained politician capable of filling his place. It is not too much to say that the Fronde would never have taken place if Richelieu had thought more of securing efficiency in those departments to which he could not give sufficient personal attention, and less of concentrating all authority in his own hands.

This concentration may have been partially forced upon Richelieu by his isolation, and by the necessity of defending his authority against jealous opponents, but it had none the less disastrous results to the administration of finance. On the fall of la Vieuville, the duties of *surintendant* were divided between Michel Marillac and Champigny, of whom the former was undoubtedly the ablest of Richelieu's colleagues, and had also a genuine de-

sire for reform. In 1626 Marillac was appointed
keeper of the seals, and the finances were intrusted
to the marquis d'Effiat. On his death in 1632 the
system of dual control was revived by the appointment of Bullion and Bouthillier, whose chief qualification was that they were the docile agents of
the cardinal, and after the former's death Bouthillier remained in office alone. These ministerial
changes are coincident with a steady decline in the
management of French finance. The short-lived
and rather half-hearted reforms belong to the period of Marillac's tenure of office. Under d'Effiat
some measure of order was preserved, and the public credit was maintained, and in some respects im-
proved, in spite of an increase of taxation. The
reckless multiplication of both exactions and of
indebtedness belongs to the time of Bullion and
Bouthillier.

There can be no doubt that Richelieu's neglect
of the paramount duty of financial reform, whether
it be condemned or excused, was of decisive
importance for the future history of France. No
subsequent minister was strong enough to cleanse
the Augean stable, and the partial improvement
effected by Colbert was soon effaced by the lavish

expenditure of Louise XIV. on luxury and war.
Throughout the eighteenth century the efforts of
France were crippled by the burden of a chronic
deficit which threatened to bring the state to bank-
ruptcy. It is impossible to exaggerate the importance to a state of a wholesome and efficient financial system. France was able to get the better of
Spain because the economic condition of Spain was
even worse than her own. But the decline of Spain
and the exhaustion of Holland left France face to
face with England, and the two states waged a
long and desperate struggle for commercial and
colonial expansion. The financial system of mediæval England, though not so full of abuses as that
of France, was almost equally inefficient and sta-
tionary. The greatest boon which the Common-
wealth conferred upon England was the abolition
of the antiquated methods of taxation, and the sub-
stitution of a system which, whatever its faults in
detail, had the supreme merit of making the national revenue proportionate to the nation's wealth.
Among the many causes which helped England to
gain the victory over France on the sea, in America
and in India, not the least important was the vast
superiority of her financial administration, which

enabled her to defray with comparative ease an expenditure which reduced her rival to exhaustion
and despair. This superiority might never have existed if Richelieu or his colleagues had been far-
sighted enough to grapple with problems from
which they deliberately turned their attention.

Although Richelieu deliberately set himself to
establish absolutism and to free the monarchy from
all effective restraints upon its action, it would be
a great error to suppose that he recklessly disre-
garded public opinion, or that he failed to appreciate the strength which any government obtains
by conciliating its support. It is true that he would
have nothing to do with the States-General, but he
summoned two important meetings of Notables,
one in 1626 to parade the national sanction of his
anti-papal action in the matter of the Valtelline,
and the other in 1627 to strengthen his domestic
position after the first conspiracy against him had
ended in the execution of Chalais. Of course these
meetings were carefully packed, and they were allowed no legislative powers. His motives for their
convention were much the same as those which induced Simon de Montfort to summon the parliament of 1265, or Philip the Fair to hold the first

sessions of the States-General. At the same time the Notables were allowed, especially in 1627, considerable latitude and liberty of discussion, and their debates gave to the measures and schemes of the government a publicity which a less enlightened despotism might have considered both dangerous and degrading.

The same desire to satisfy and gain over opinion is apparent in his patronage of literature, though here personal tastes and interests combined to influence his action. He surrounded himself with a small regiment of learned scribes, whom he employed to produce treatises in support of his views on such subjects as the claims of the crown to foreign territories, or the proper relations of church and state. The *Memoirs* and the *Succincte Narration*, which constitute his own chief contributions to literature, were probably drafted in the first instance by these subordinates, though he reserved the task of revision for himself. But his interest was by no means confined to the serious and practical uses of literary composition. He was himself an indefatigable writer of versified dramas, though his industry could not command success nor his authority applause. His personal failure, however, did not

make him meanly jealous of more fortunate followers of the Muses. Nearly all the most prominent
writers of the day were in personal intercourse
with him, and were in receipt of pensions or gra-
tuities from his purse. The two greatest prose
writers, Voiture and Balzac, repaid his liberality
by eulogising his administration in terms of equal
warmth and sincerity. It is true that the patronage
of an absolute ruler, whether king or minister, is
not always an unmixed benefit to literature, and
that none of Richelieu's *protégés*, except Corneille,
can be placed in the highest rank. But on the other
hand court patronage in France did effect a very
notable literary revival, and it is impossible to deny
to Richelieu some credit for the rise of the next
generation of authors, whose works have reflected
such glory upon the France of Louis XIV.

In connection with literature Richelieu will always be best remembered as the founder of the
French Academy. This had its origin in the private
meetings of a number of literary friends, who in
1629 formed the habit of assembling once a week
for the discussion of literary topics and the consideration of each other's productions. These meetings had already been going on for four years when

Richelieu was informed of them by one of the numerous busybodies whose function it was to tell him of everything that was going on in Paris. With characteristic keenness, though foreign affairs seemed sufficiently critical to absorb all his energies, he grasped the possible uses of such an organisation, and offered the members a constitution under government patronage. There was some natural hesitation, as party spirit ran high in France, and men of letters were by no means unanimously cardinalist. But the offer could not be safely or courteously refused, and letters-patent were drawn up in 1635, though the bigoted opposition of the parliament, ever jealous of new corporations, delayed their formal promulgation till July 10, 1637. The primary function of the Academy was to regulate and purify the French language, to make it the most perfect of modern tongues, and to "render it not only elegant, but also capable of treating all the arts and all the sciences." But from the first both the founder's intentions and the habits of the members combined to give it a second function as a tribunal of literary criticism. Richelieu himself pointed clearly to this duty by demanding in 1637 a corporate opinion on Corneille's *Cid*, which had been attacked in the *Observations* of Scudéry. From this time it became a regular part of the Academy's business to criticise, and, if it thought fit, to express formal approbation of the works both of members and others; and it needs only a superficial knowledge of French literature to appreciate what an immense influence it has thus exerted both upon language and style.

From the political point of view the origin of French journalism is even more important than the foundation of the Academy, and to this also Richelieu gave the deciding impulse. Hitherto the only newspaper in France had been an annual publication, the *Mercure françois*, which was a continuation of the *Chronologie septénaire* of Palma Cayet. This was obviously insufficient to satisfy the growing interest in political events, and it was supplemented by a number of unauthorised fly-sheets, called *nouvelles à la main*, which were circulated either in print or manuscript, and eagerly read. The most industrious compiler of news was a prominent physician, Théophraste Renaudot, who supplied *nouvelles* for the distraction as well as medicines for the cure of his wealthy patients. Renaudot succeeded in gaining the confidence of

Richelieu, and in 1631 received a formal license to transform his fugitive fly-sheets into a regular newspaper under government sanction. Thus was founded the *Gazette,* or, as it was called later, the *Gazette de la France.* It appeared weekly in a small quarto sheet of four pages, each containing a single column. From the first the extent and accuracy of its intelligence gave it a secure pre-eminence over any rival publication, and its circulation and importance rapidly increased. Both king and minister were among the contributors to its pages, and Louis XIII. took a special pleasure in the labour of composition and revision. Secure of this novel method of influencing opinion, Richelieu was able to dispense for the rest of his ministry with the more cumbrous system of assembling Notables which he had adopted at starting. In the words of Henri Martin, he had "given birth to the two great enemies, whose struggle was to fill the modern world —absolutism and the press."

CHAPTER IX

RICHELIEU AND THE CHURCH

RICHELIEU, although a bishop and a cardinal, was not a great theologian, nor was he in the narrowest sense a great churchman. Many of his contemporaries, endowed with far less dignity and authority, yet exercised an incomparably more distinct and vital influence on the religious life of his time than he can claim to have done. Still his career is coincident with a very important epoch in the history of the French Church, and both in his actions and in his *Memoirs* he shows a very keen interest in ecclesiastical matters, and a very vivid sense of their importance to the order and wellbeing of the state. Possibly his interest was rather that of the politician than of the ecclesiastic, but it was none the less real, nor was the influence which he could not fail to possess diminished because he himself was lacking

in spiritual insight or because his motives were
rather secular than religious. These considerations
make it impossible, even in a brief sketch like the
present, to dismiss his relations with the Church in
a brief and perfunctory paragraph.

The sixteenth century had witnessed two of the
greatest religious movements in history. The first
was the Reformation, by which a number of states,
mostly in Northern Europe, threw off all dependence upon Rome, and adopted religious doctrines
and organisation more or less at variance with those
which had hitherto prevailed throughout Western
Christendom. By the second or Counter Reformation, the Roman Catholic Church profited by the
lessons it had received, reformed the abuses which
had provoked discontent and rebellion, and strengthened its internal organisation in order not only
to prevent further defections, but also to recover
some of the ground that had been lost. This re-
forming movement, which was immensely stimulated by the efforts of the Jesuit order, found its
final expression in the decrees of the Council of
Trent. But although France was represented at
Trent, and although the doctrinal definitions of
the council were welcomed, yet those decrees which

touched the constitution of the Church and restored discipline were never accepted or promul-
gated in France. There were two primary motives
for this repudiation of the chief measures of reform. The crown contended that the conciliar
decrees diminished the authority and patronage conferred upon the kings by the Concordat of 1516.
The Parliament of Paris complained that they
would destroy the liberties of the Gallican Church,
which had always been dear to the official classes
since their first definition in the Pragmatic Sanction of Bourges in 1438.

Thus the Church of France remained unre-
formed, and during the religious wars the abuses
of the old system become still more numerous and
conspicuous. Many archbishoprics and bishoprics
were allowed to remain vacant, while others were
held by men who had obtained them by uncanon-
ical or simoniacal means. Most of the bishops were
non-resident and neglected their dioceses. Du Vair,
who lived at Aix as first president of the Parliament
of Provence, was bishop of Lisieux, in Normandy,
which he never visited. It is recorded that on one
occasion the bishop of St. Malo confirmed two
thousand persons in a single village, which proves

that his visits cannot have been very frequent. There were no schools for the education of the clergy, most of whom were extremely ignorant and incompetent. While the revenues of the church were very large, the village *curés* were lamentably ill-paid, and their mode of life was practically that of the peasants from whom they were sprung, and whom they were vainly expected to elevate and instruct. The fabric of the churches was in a lamentable state. Many had been used as fortresses in the war, with very natural results; others had been profaned or destroyed by the Huguenots. In many parishes divine service had come to an end altogether, and the people were left without any religious ministrations. And if the condition of the secular clergy was bad, that of the regulars was still worse. The headships of religious houses were frequently given to children or to persons of scandalous character. In many cases the abbot was a layman, who drew the revenues of the monastery, while his duties were discharged by an ill-paid substitute. The count of Soissons was said to receive an ecclesiastical revenue of 100,000 livres a year, while his place was filled by a prior with an annual income of 1000. Elsewhere the revenues, both of

monasteries and of bishoprics, were saddled with
pensions and reserves which had been granted to
courtiers of both sexes. Discipline was completely
neglected, and both monks and nuns lived worldly,
self-indulgent, and often vicious lives.

The termination of the religious wars by the accession of Henry IV. and his acceptance of the
Roman Catholic faith was followed by a notable
religious revival in France, which reached its zenith
during Richelieu's ministry. But this revival was
not the work of the state, nor even of the Church
acting in its corporate capacity. The whole credit
belongs to a few devoted and highly-gifted individuals, whose lives will always attract attention
and admiration as long as the record of religious
enthusiasm and heroic self-sacrifice awakens any
responsive chord in the hearts of mankind. The
dominant impulse was given by a native of Savoy,
St. François de Sales, but the most active and influential worker was a Frenchman, the famous St.
Vincent de Paul. As was natural, the revival was
a composite and many-sided movement. One of its
manifestations was a general desire among the
clergy to strengthen the bonds which connected
France with the Universal Church, of which she

professed to be the eldest daughter. This Ultramontane tendency was specially encouraged by the
Jesuits, who had been restored to France in 1604
after a brief period of exile, and at once gained
great influence at court by supplying a series of
royal confessors. Another sign of the revival was
the endeavour of the Church to free itself from
the trammels of state control, to recover as much
as possible the free election of its own dignitaries,
and, above all, to restore the independence of clerical judicature, which had been much restricted by
the encroachments of the secular courts, and especially by the practice of appealing on purely
clerical matters from the Church courts to the
Parliament of Paris (the famous *appel comme
d'abus*). But by far the most conspicuous and
creditable aspect of the movement was its practical side, the immense energy and enthusiasm
that was thrown into the work of active charity, of
education, and of monastic reform.

The Roman Catholic Church has always shown
itself honourably conscious of its duties towards
the poor and afflicted, but at no time and place has
it undertaken the task of charitable relief with
more devotion than in the early part of the seven-

teenth century. It was upon pious women that the task was mainly thrown, and among the numerous orders that were founded to systematise and encourage their labours two are specially conspicuous for the piety of their founders and for their subsequent development. The Visitandines, or Congregation of the Visitation, were founded at Annecy by François de Sales, and a branch was established in Paris in 1621 by Madame de Chantal. In the eighteenth century the order possessed more than a hundred houses in France. Still more famous and useful have been the *Sœurs de la Charité*, or Gray Sisters, founded and organised by Vincent de Paul in 1633, and rapidly extended under the headship of Madame Legras. This organisation—for it can hardly be called an order—was mainly composed of women of humble origin, whose habits and training fitted them for the toilsome and often repulsive labours which they undertook. At the same time Vincent de Paul succeeded in enlisting in the good work many ladies of the highest rank, who, with the title of *Dames de la Charité*, undertook the task of organising relief, and acting as visitors and overseers of the humbler Sisters. So great was their success, according to an admiring biographer

of the founder, that in the first year of their activity no less than 760 heretics were converted to
the orthodox faith. Prominent among these ladies
was Richelieu's favourite niece, Madame de Combalet, afterwards duchess d'Aiguillon, and it was
she who succeeded in enlisting her uncle's sympathy and support in a work which he probably
thought outside the duties of the state, and which
he had little time or inclination to direct in person.

Almost equally numerous were the associations
formed for the education and training of the
clergy. Here the lead was taken by de Bérulle, who
founded the *Oratoire de Jésus* in 1611, and obtained its approval from Paul V. in 1613. Within
a brief period the Oratorians possessed no less than
fifty houses, and among their pupils were such men
as Malebranche, Mascaron, and Massillon. De
Bérulle found numerous imitators, of whom the
chief were Adrien Bourdoise, the founder of the
seminary of St. Nicolas du Chardonnet, and Jean
Jacques Olier, who organised in 1641 the celebrated
seminary of St. Sulpice. But in the work of clerical
education, as in that of charity, by far the most
successful and practical organiser was Vincent de
Paul. The Congregation of the Mission was founded

by him in 1625 in the Collège des Bons Enfants, and in 1632, when it received formal confirmation from Urban VIII., was moved into more spacious quarters in the Priory of St. Lazare, whence its members obtained the name of *Lazaristes*. The success of this institution in raising the standard of piety and priestly activity throughout the country districts was marvellous, and attracted the interested attention of Richelieu. In an interview with Vincent de Paul he asked for full information as to the aims and constitution of the order, and gave it solid encouragement by recommending its more prominent members for ecclesiastical promotion.

Nor was the work of secular education neglected in the general revival of clerical enthusiasm. The Congregation of the Ursulines, founded in Italy in the previous century, was now introduced into France by Madeleine Lhuillier, and devoted itself with marked success to the teaching of girls. But by far the greatest educating force was supplied by the Jesuits. The edict for their restoration in 1604 allowed them to possess thirteen colleges in the provinces, but they were at first excluded from the capital. This obstacle was overcome by the influence of the king's confessor, Father Cotton, and in 1609 they were permitted to give public instruction in the Collège de Clermont. This gave rise to a long and bitter struggle between the Jesuits and the University of Paris, in which the former only held their own through the unwavering support of Richelieu. He had little sympathy with the Jesuits, who were opposed both to his foreign policy and to much of his home government, but he realised that in education, if not in commerce, a monopoly is a dangerous gift to a corporation. Thanks to his support, the pupils of the Order in 1627 numbered no fewer than 13,195. This strenuous competition was wholesome to the University itself, which at last abandoned the effort to suppress its rivals, and set to work to recover its declining influence by improving its own methods of instruction.

If Richelieu's attitude towards the work of charity and education was passive rather than active, he took a more direct interest in the furtherance of monastic reform. This holds a prominent place among the proposals which he submitted to the king in 1625, and throughout his ministry he endeavoured by frequent visitations to enforce the observance of the stricter rules of monastic life. To increase his authority for this purpose he obtained his own nomination as general of the great orders of Cluny, Citeaux, and the Premonstratensians, in spite of the opposition of the pope, who refused to confirm him in the two latter offices. But the magistrates and other secular agents whom Richelieu employed provoked ecclesiastical jealousy and opposition, and in the end a great deal more was effected by individual initiative than by government intervention. By far the greatest achievements of the period were the foundation of the reformed Benedictine Congregation of St. Maur, whence proceeded in the next generation the monumental works of French erudition, and the restoration of discipline in the nunneries of Port Royal and Maubuisson by the famous Angelique Arnauld. From Port Royal nuns were despatched on missions to extend the work of reform to all the convents of France. But if Richelieu's share in the movement was less predominant than he probably anticipated, yet his example and patronage contributed to the success of the efforts of others, and he may further claim the credit of having terminated the long warfare between regulars and seculars. By the decision of a conference which he initiated, and whose labours he personally superintended, the jealousy

with which the parish priests had always regarded
the intervention of their rivals was at last allayed.
The monks were subjected to episcopal authority,
and they were only allowed to preach and receive
confession with the express permission of the ordinary.

So far the ecclesiastical revival had proceeded
with Richelieu's approval, and to some extent with
his active encouragement and support. But with
the Ultramontane tendencies of the movement he
came into direct and hostile collision. During the
minority of Louis XIII. the support of Mary de
Medici had enabled cardinal du Perron and the
Ultramontane party in France to gain a considerable increase of strength. This was conclusively
proved by the removal of Richer, the chief champion of Gallican liberties, from his office of Syndic
in the Sorbonne, by the frustration of the Parliament's attack on the Jesuits, and by the attitude assumed by the clerical estate in the States-General.
But this progress was checked by the accession of
Richelieu to power. With his strong sense of the
overpowering importance of national interests, he
was not likely to be submissive to a foreign authority, whose action could not possibly be dictated by

a single-minded regard for France. Among his early measures the expulsion of papal troops from the Valtelline and the conclusion of the treaty of 1626 with the Huguenots excited the horrified animosity of the Roman Catholic world. Bitter attacks were published against the "cardinal of the Huguenots," the betrayer of his Church to the infidels, and Richelieu thought it necessary to procure a condemnation of these libels from a clerical synod. It was at this juncture that a book reached Paris from Rome, written by a Jesuit, Sanctarellus, and approved both by the pope and the General of the Order. In this book, "the most evil of its kind," as Richelieu calls it, were maintained in their most extreme form the doctrines of papal absolutism: "the pope may punish and depose kings, not only for heresy and schism, but for any intolerable offence, for incapacity or for negligence; he has power to admonish kings and to punish them with death; all princes who govern states do so by commission from His Holiness, who may claim to govern them himself, etc." These maxims, says Richelieu, are capable of ruining the whole Church, and they are the more preposterous with regard to the pope, as he "is a temporal prince, and has made no such renunciation of earthly greatness as to be indifferent to it." He hastened to stimulate the Gallican sentiment in opposition to such teaching. The Sorbonne, or theological faculty of the University, censured the book as "containing novel, false, and erroneous doctrines, contrary to the word of God, and rendering odious the dignity of the sovereign Pontiff." The parliament ordered the book to be publicly burned, and eagerly seized the opportunity to renew their attack upon the Jesuits, whom they proposed to expel from their colleges, and even from France. Richelieu, however, interfered to check their ardour, in the belief that "it was necessary to reduce the Jesuits to such a state that they had no power to be harmful, but not to drive them to attempt any mischief from despair." The Order escaped further persecution by accepting a solemn declaration that they repudiated the doctrines of Sanctarellus about the power of kings, that they acknowledged that kings hold immediately of God, and that they would never teach any doctrines on this matter other than those held by the clergy, the Universities of the kingdom, and the Sorbonne.

This alliance of Richelieu with the Gallican

party could not but be distasteful to the papal court, and it was by no means obliterated by subsequent services, such as the taking of La Rochelle, and the strengthening of the temporal power of the papacy by the anti-Spanish policy pursued in the Mantuan succession. On the strength of these services Richelieu ventured to demand a boon for which he was extremely eager—that he should be appointed papal legate in France, as cardinal Amboise had been in the reign of Louis XII. But Urban VIII. had no mind to give increased power to a prelate who was already sufficiently independent, and it is possible that Richelieu's leniency to the Huguenots was in some measure a retaliation for this refusal. Nor were his other requests more favourably received. Urban refused to make him legate in Avignon, to allow his nomination as coadjutor of the archbishop of Trier, and to confirm him as general of the three great monastic orders. The cardinal's hat was never granted to Father Joseph, in spite of the persistent efforts of the French government; and the pope steadfastly declined to recognise the validity of the decision which pronounced the marriage of Gaston with Margaret of Lorraine to be null and void.

These continued rebuffs, and especially the last, inspired Richelieu with the wish to teach the pope a lesson. Pierre Dupuy, one of the ablest of the authors whose learning was always at the cardinal's command, drew up an exhaustive treatise on the *Libertés de l'Eglise Gallicane*, which stated fully the arguments not only against papal despotism, but also for the subjection of the church to the state. This book, which was published anonymously in 1638, caused the greatest sensation both in France and at Rome, and the council found it advisable to decree its suppression, though only on the technical ground that it had been published without license. But the book continued to be sold, and in the next year the execution of an attendant of the French envoy at Rome gave rise to an open quarrel. The envoy, d'Estrées, ceased all communications with the Vatican. Louis XIII. closed his doors to the papal nuncio in Paris, and forbade the bishops to hold any intercourse with him. It was currently reported that Richelieu was prepared to break off all connection with Rome and to obtain from a national synod his own election as patriarch of France. A priest named Hersent hastened to denounce the projected schism in a treatise

which he published under the title of *Optatus
Gallus*. The bishops did not venture to defend the
book, and the parliament hastened to proscribe
it, and indirectly to express approval of the doctrines of Dupuy. But the pope could not afford to
carry any further his quarrel with France. Satisfaction was given to d'Estrées, and the grant of a
cardinal's hat to Mazarin, who acted as papal envoy
on the occasion, was taken as the pledge of reconciliation. But Urban VIII. never forgave the prelate who had humbled him. On Richelieu's death he
refused to allow the usual commemorative service
for a cardinal to be celebrated at Rome, and he is
said to have expressed his opinion of the dead statesman's character in terms which sounded oddly in
the mouth of a pope: "If there is a God, he will pay
dearly for his conduct; but if there is no God, then
he was truly an admirable man."

Although Richelieu was the champion of Gallican liberties against papal pretensions, he was
equally resolute to enforce the duties of the clergy
to the state. In this respect his conduct as a minister
stands in instructive contrast to the more purely
clerical attitude which he had assumed at the meeting of the States-General. In his speech as orator

of the clergy he had made the following claims for
his order: (1) the more frequent admission of
ecclesiastics to office and to the royal council; (2)
the prohibition of future grants of church revenues
to laymen, either directly or by way of pensions
and reserves; (3) the release of the clergy from
direct taxes, on the ground that the only tribute
which they owed was their prayers; (4) the restoration of clerical jurisdiction to its former limits
and independence; (5) the recognition of the decrees of the Council of Trent. Of these demands
the only one which he gratified when the opportunity came was the first. His partiality for ecclesiastical agents, not only in diplomacy, but in military
and naval commands, was a subject of derision in
Europe, and gave a handle against him to the pope,
who openly expressed his disapproval of the employment of churchmen, like the cardinal de la
Valette, in leading armies to the field. The other
proposals proved nothing more than pious wishes.
The Council of Trent remained unacknowledged.
The diversion of ecclesiastical revenues to laymen
continued, and Richelieu himself is said to have rewarded a favourite fiddler with the gift of an
abbey. No limit was placed on the encroachment of

the secular courts on church jurisdiction, nor on the employment of the *appel comme d'abus*. And the question of clerical taxation gave rise to an open and envenomed quarrel between Richelieu and his fellow-clergy.

The revenues of the French clergy, whether from land or from other sources, were wholly exempt from direct taxation. The clerical assemblies were in the habit of making an annual grant of 2,000,000 livres, but they always protested that this was a *don gratuit* and not a compulsory payment, and, moreover, such a sum was ludicrously out of proportion to the wealth of the Church. Among the financial expedients forced upon Richelieu by military expenses were increased demands on the liberality of the Church synods, and these were usually granted, though always with murmuring and reluctance. But in 1640 he came forward with a wholly novel and unforeseen demand. His supporter and confidant, the bishop of Chartres, had collected documents from the royal archives to prove that land could only be held in mortmain by letters-patent, to be obtained on payment of a *droit d'amortissement*. This form the clergy had systematically failed to observe, and therefore it

The same determination to prevent Gallicanism from developing into a claim for clerical independence, and to enforce at all hazards the solidarity and authority of the state, is visible in Richelieu's relations with one of his most famous contemporaries, the Abbé de St. Cyran. St. Cyran had not yet become the founder of a sect, but he was already famous as the reputed author of *Petrus Aurelius*, and as a formidable free-lance on the side of Gallican liberties. His piety and learning gave him an influence quite out of proportion to his ecclesiastical rank: he was the spiritual director of Port Royal, which had been transferred by Angelique Arnauld to Paris, and he was the confidential adviser of many distinguished persons of both sexes. St. Cyran's conception of the Church as an oligarchy of bishops rather than a monarchy brought him into collision with Rome, and both he and his friend Jansen had been from the first hostile critics of the principles and morality of Jesuit teaching. Both these positions commended themselves to Richelieu, who was engaged in a quarrel with the papacy, and had good reason to dislike the Ultramontane and Spanish predilections of the Jesuits. In his early days he had been brought into intimate relations with St. Cyran, through their common friend the bishop of Poitiers, and he now made strenuous efforts to gain the allegiance of the man whom he openly declared to be the most learned theologian in Europe. No less than five bishoprics —some say eight—were successively offered to the friend of his youth. But St. Cyran resolutely refused to sacrifice his independence by accepting preferment from a "government which only wished for slaves." The autocracy, which he suspected Richelieu of a desire to establish, was quite as repugnant to his principles as the absolutism of the pope. His obstinate self-confidence and isolation were the first cause of Richelieu's enmity. The higher his appreciation of St. Cyran's ability, the more he mistrusted the growth of an influence which was outside his control. And to this first ground of alienation others were speedily added. We have seen what importance Richelieu attached to the dissolution of Gaston's marriage with Margaret of Lorraine. On this subject St. Cyran did not hesitate to take the same line as Urban VIII., and to declare that it was impious to annul a sacrament of the Church for purely political reasons. But probably the greatest displeasure was caused by the action of Jansen, of whose teaching St. Cyran was already the avowed champion. Jansen, a native of the Spanish Netherlands, had published the *Mars Gallicus*, in which he bitterly denounced the conduct of France in betraying the cause of Roman Catholicism by an open alliance with Lutherans and Calvinists. This pamphlet, which earned from the Spanish government the elevation of its author to the bishopric of Ypres, appeared in a French translation in 1638. Richelieu was always keenly sensitive to such attacks on his policy, and as he could not touch the chief culprit, he determined to take vengeance on the disciple. In May 1638 St. Cyran was arrested and imprisoned in Vincennes, where he remained till the cardinal's death. His papers were seized, and a judicial inquiry instituted, in the hope of obtaining evidence for a charge of heresy, but the scheme resulted in failure, and the prisoner was never brought to trial. That Richelieu foresaw the formation of a Jansenist sect as the inevitable result of St. Cyran's combination of personal independence with deep spiritual influence over others is proved by his comparing him with the great reformers of the previous century. "If Luther and Calvin," he said, "had been imprisoned when they began to dogmatise, the states of Europe would have been spared many troubles." Later, when the prince of Condé tried to obtain the prisoner's release, he replied, "Do you know the man you are speaking of? he is more dangerous than six armies." But the cardinal's harshness towards an innocent opponent was subtly avenged by the famous John of Werth. He had been a captive since the battle of Rheinfelden, and had made St. Cyran's acquaintance in their common prison of Vincennes. The general was brought from his confinement to witness the sumptuous presentation of Richelieu's comedy of *Miriame* before the king and court. When asked for his opinion of the spectacle, he replied that it was magnificent, but that what astounded him most was to find "in the Most Christian kingdom, the bishops at the comedy and the saints in prison." Richelieu pretended not to hear, but the blow must have struck shrewdly home.

It is impossible to discover in Richelieu's relations with the Church any signs that he was actuated by profound convictions or overmastering principles. Though he made use of parties, he belonged to none. In ecclesiastical matters, as contrasted with politics, he was an opportunist pure and simple. If the pope had not refused his demands, and tried to thwart his schemes, he would never have identified himself with the advocates of Gallicanism. So long as Gallican liberties existed in practice he had no desire that they should be defined or formally recognised. When an open quarrel with Rome broke out, his haughty and stubborn temper doubtless prompted him to carry it through after the fashion of Henry VIII., and to establish the patriarchate which his enemies accused him of coveting. But his temper rarely got the better of his discretion. He was keen-sighted enough to apprehend the differences, both of history and opinion, which rendered the action of England no safe guide for France, and he foresaw that a final rupture with the papacy would produce such a ferment that the political influence of his country would be annihilated for at least half a century. Again, he was far too thoroughly imbued with the spirit of his order to be a consistent and thoroughgoing Erastian. If the clergy had not been always suspicious of his Protestant alliances, and often sympathetic with the enemies of France, he would never have stirred a step from his way to attack their corporate privileges and independence.

It was this detachment from religious partisanship which enabled him to subordinate ecclesiastical to political considerations, and to be the first European statesman who ventured to translate the principles of toleration into practice. His attitude in this respect is the more remarkable when we remember that he was no eighteenth century sceptic, confident in human powers and doubtful of divine intervention. If Richelieu profoundly influenced his age, it was not because he was before it, but because he so thoroughly identified himself with it. It would be misleading to call him a religious man, but he was certainly superstitious. His private letters furnish plentiful evidence of his belief in astrology, in magic, and in the small popular prejudices against unlucky days and actions. This vein of superstition—not uncommon in great men of action—merits the more attention, because without it it would be impossible to plead any defence for Richelieu in an episode which looms very largely in the pages of his detractors—the case of Urbain Grandier. The story itself is sufficiently remarkable, and though the evidence has now been fully published, there are several questions connected with the case which it is difficult to answer with absolute certainty.

Urbain Grandier was a priest of Loudun in
Poitou, of a handsome and imposing exterior, and
possessed of great influence over women, which he
almost certainly abused. In one way and another he
had excited the enmity of several prominent inhabitants of the town, who brought against him a
charge of immorality and impiety. In the court
of the bishop of Poitiers he was condemned, but
on appeal the sentence was reversed both by the
présidial of Poitiers and by the archbishop of Bordeaux. Grandier's too obvious exultation in his triumph redoubled the fury of his opponents, who
were eager to find some new means of procuring his
ruin. One of them, Mignon, was director of the
Ursuline convent in Loudun. Rumours began to
spread that some of the nuns were possessed with
devils, that they were afflicted with extraordinary
bodily contortions, and that in their ravings they
brought grave charges against Grandier. The director and other priests were called in to exorcise
the demons, and they reported that they obtained
from the mouths of the latter a reluctant confession as to the master who had sent them. Still no
formal charge was brought, and opinion in Loudun
was divided between Grandier's accusers and de-

fenders. As before, the bishop of Poitiers was on one side, professed his belief in the evidence, while the archbishop of Bordeaux was incredulous. It was at this juncture that a commissioner of the government, Laubardemont, came to Loudun to superintend the destruction of the castle. He was a confidential agent of Richelieu, and was subsequently employed to collect evidence against St. Cyran. The popularity of a professed spy and informer was not likely to be great, and his reputation has consequently suffered. Laubardemont was completely gained over by the stories of Grandier's accusers. He undertook to bring the whole matter before the cardinal, and he is said to have prejudiced him against the accused by asserting that Grandier was the author of a scurrilous libel, *Le Cordonnier de Loudun*, that had been circulated when Richelieu was a resident in Poitou as bishop of Luçon. The result was that a special commission of fourteen persons, with Laubardemont at its head, was appointed to try the case. The trial itself was, from a modern point of view, farcical, the bias of the court was unmistakable, and the evidence was mainly that which the exorcists professed to have extracted from the so-called devils. Grandier was

sentenced to death, tortured to make him confess
his accomplices, and finally burned under circumstances of exceptional and wanton barbarity.

That Grandier's death was a judicial murder of
the worst kind, and that fraud as well as credulity
entered into the conduct of the case against him, is
incontestable. But it is by no means easy to dis-
tribute equally the exact measures of guilt. That
the whole affair was a gigantic conspiracy, in
which nuns, priests, the bishop of Poitiers, and
many others played preconcerted parts to destroy
a common enemy, is preposterous. The very length
of time—two years—during which the professed
marvels were prolonged is conclusive against such
extensive and well-organised complicity. The
further assertion of Gui Patin that Richelieu was
at the bottom of the plot, and that he resorted to
such an elaborate imposture to ruin a humble but
detested libeller, is not only absurd in itself, but
runs counter to all that we know of the cardinal's
open, if often excessive, malevolence. The proba-
bility is that the nuns suffered from religious hys-
teria, of which there are many recorded instances
in the same period of revival, and that the suggestions of their spiritual director led them to make

their incoherent charges against the priest whom he was known to detest, and of whom they had doubtless heard much that was evil. Some, at any rate, of the exorcists were men whose character raises them above the charge of deliberate ill-faith. All that can be urged against Richelieu is that he saw no *a priori* difficulties as to the credibility of the accusations, and that he allowed the machinery of a special commission, always more likely to look for guilt than for innocence, to be employed in a case where there was no possible justification for its use.

CHAPTER X

RICHELIEU'S LAST YEARS
1641–1642

RICHELIEU did not live to witness the conclusion of the great war in which France had engaged under his auspices. The treaties of Westphalia and the Pyrenees, especially the latter, might have been concluded earlier if his life had been prolonged, but in spite of the delay he is as much their author as if he had signed the actual documents. In fact, all the substantial advantages which France gained by these treaties had been practically secured by 1640. The military events of the next two years did little but render more certain the ultimate triumph of France. In 1641 the flowing tide of French successes seemed for a moment to be arrested. In Italy and in Artois the French troops had enough to do to hold their own. Charles of Lorraine was restored, only to prove once more a traitor to his promises, and his duchy had to be re-occupied before the year was over. In Germany Guébriant defeated the Imperialists at Wolfenbüttel, but the death of Baner and other causes prevented the allies from gaining any important results by their success. In 1642, however, the French cause made rapid and decisive strides. In Italy the princes Thomas and Maurice deserted the Spaniards to join their sister-in-law, and their adhesion turned the balance decisively in favour of the French. A great effort was planned by Richelieu on the side of the Pyrenees, and the capture of Perpignan and Salces completed the second and final union of Roussillon to France. In Germany Guébriant opened the year with a decisive victory at Kempten, and this was followed by a campaign in which Torstenson, Baner's successor, emulated the most brilliant achievements of Gustavus Adolphus. By a series of rapid and masterly movements this general, though imprisoned in his litter by gout, overran Silesia and Moravia, and caused a panic in Vienna. Compelled to retreat by superior forces, he threw himself into Saxony and laid siege to Leipzig. When the Imperialists advanced to relieve the city, he crushed them on the plain of Breitenfeld (Nov. 2, 1642), where Gustavus Adolphus, eleven years before, had won the first great victory which established his own reputation and marked a decisive turning-point in the history of the war. The surrender of Leipzig was the reward of Torstenson's success, and the news of this brilliant triumph must have brought some consolation to Richelieu as he lay on his deathbed.

The enemies of France did not require the lessons of 1642 to teach them that little hope remained for them in arms. They had already realised that their only chance of recovering from their reverses lay in the overthrow by domestic treason of the minister whom they regarded as the author of all their misfortunes. In spite of the glory which his administration had brought to France, Richelieu had still many enemies who longed for his overthrow, and few adherents who would make strenuous efforts for his defence. Probably his best friend—though few suspected it, and perhaps the cardinal himself as little as the general public—was the king. The private letters of Louis XIII., in these two years, prove that he was not devoid of gratitude and even affection towards the man who had made his reign illustrious, though the coldness of his manner and a certain peevish resentment of anything like dictation misled even those in his most immediate confidence into a belief that it was no impossible task to alienate the king from the minister. Richelieu had ever to be on his guard against secret foes at court, who were far more dangerous than his avowed opponents. Among the latter the most prominent was the count of Soissons, who had never forgiven his defeat of 1636. He had been living ever since in the border fortress of Sedan, whence he carried on incessant intrigues with foreign states, with malcontents at home, and with the nobles who had followed the queen-mother into exile. In 1641 the young duke of Guise arrived in Sedan, and discussed with Soissons and Bouillon, the governor of the fortress, the organisation of an armed rebellion for Richelieu's overthrow. The cardinal, informed of their projects, sent orders to Bouillon to withdraw his hospitality from Soissons, and to the latter to depart for Venice. This message was the signal for civil war. The conspirators threw off all disguise and applied for aid to Spain and Austria, who were only too glad to encourage a movement which could not fail to serve their ends. The king on his side declared

Soissons, Guise, and Bouillon enemies of the state, and despatched the marshal de Châtillon to combine with the restored duke of Lorraine in an attack on Sedan. But Charles of Lorraine had already decided to break his recent treaty with France, and Châtillon was forced to stand on the defensive against the rebels, who received the aid of an Imperialist detachment under Lamboy. Their forces had already quitted Sedan and crossed the Meuse when they were attacked by the royal troops at La Marfée. It was generally anticipated that the first conflict would have decisive results, and that a victory of the insurgents would be followed by a movement on the part of Richelieu's opponents at the court and in Paris. But good fortune was on the cardinal's side, and the forecast, shrewd as it was, proved fallacious. No victory could have been more decisive. The royalist cavalry had been tampered with, and the infantry, left to itself, fled in panic-stricken confusion. But in the turmoil Soissons was killed by a chance bullet, and the death of the rebel leader, whose rank as a prince of the blood made him indispensable, deprived his confederates of all the fruits of their success. The whole scheme of rebellion was at an end. Guise fled to Brussels,

Bouillon submitted and was pardoned, and their secret sympathisers at court had to wait for a more favourable opportunity, only too pleased that they had not betrayed themselves by a premature movement.

Gratitude, as Richelieu had good reason to know, is rarely a permanent force in politics, and the most active and resolute of his opponents at court was a young man who owed his advancement entirely to the cardinal. Henri d'Effiat, marquis de Cinq-Mars, was the son of the marquis d'Effiat, who had been for four years superintendent of finance, but had won more renown as a military leader. Richelieu had brought Cinq-Mars to the notice of Louis XIII. at a moment when he wished to divert the king's interest from the society of Mademoiselle d'Hautefort, to whom Louis's platonic affections had returned after the retirement of Louise de la Fayette. The move was successful in gaining its immediate end. Good looks and an attractive manner gained for Cinq-Mars the favour of the king, and he was speedily advanced to the office of grand equerry. But this rapid promotion turned his head. The pleasures and magnificence of the court failed to satisfy him, and he aspired to the rank of duke and peer, to military distinction, and to political ascendency. Richelieu saw clearly that he must resign all hope of using Cinq-Mars as a submissive tool, and he consoled himself for his disappointment by ruthlessly snubbing his youthful ambitions. His pretensions to the hand of Marie de Gonzaga, afterwards queen of Poland, were treated as a piece of ridiculous presumption. His endeavour to remain in attendance on Louis at meetings of the council, and even at personal conferences between the king and minister, was resented as a gross impertinence. Like most young men, Cinq-Mars could endure anything better than contempt, and he became the bitter enemy of his former patron. Confident in his secure hold of the king's affection, he resolved to play the part of a Luynes, vainly hoping that Richelieu would be as easily got rid of as Concini had been.

Cinq-Mars had been an accomplice in the conspiracy of Soissons, and had been terribly frightened by its sudden collapse. But his courage returned when he found that his complicity was undiscovered, and he resumed the schemes which had been for a moment interrupted. His chief confidant was François de Thou, a son of the famous

historian, who had enjoyed and then forfeited the
favour of Richelieu. He seems to have been
genuinely convinced that his inconstant employer
was the oppressor of France and the wanton dis-
turber of the peace of Europe. Cinq-Mars had for
a time entertained the idea of assassination as the
best method of removing his enemy, but de Thou,
more upright if less thoroughgoing, persuaded him
to abstain from crime and to adhere to the well-
worn methods of conspiracy. In order to gain a
refuge and a rallying point, in case armed rebellion
became imperative, de Thou was sent to gain over
the veteran intriguer, Bouillon, who was still in
possession of the invaluable stronghold of Sedan.
As a prince of the blood was deemed indispensable
to serve as a figure-head for the rebels, overtures
were made to Gaston of Orleans, who had been living in tranquil obscurity since the birth of a
dauphin had reduced him to comparative insignificance. Bouillon, distrusting the strength of purely
native effort, insisted on the necessity of foreign
assistance. In spite of the opposition of de Thou,
who had unusual scruples about embarking in obvious treason, Fontrailles, another friend of Cinq-
Mars, was despatched to procure the support of

Spain, on condition that when peace should be made after the accomplishment of the *coup d'état* all French conquests in the war should be surrendered. In the meantime no efforts were to be spared by the favourite to detach Louis from Richelieu's influence, and to convince the king that his own comfort, the prosperity of France, and the peace of Europe required the cardinal's dismissal as an indispensable condition.

On his side Richelieu, of all statesmen the best served by his spies, was by no means blind to the dangers which threatened him. He had made a last effort to disarm Cinq-Mars and to remove him from the court by offering him the government of Touraine. The offer was refused, and from that moment there was open war between the two men. But there was as yet no evidence sufficient to convince Louis XIII. of the treasonable designs of his favourite, and until that could be obtained the struggle resolved itself into a duel for the dominant influence over the king; and for this the two rivals seemed to outside observers not unequally matched.

But if they appeared equally matched in one respect, in others the contrast was complete and

striking. Cinq-Mars was in the prime of youthful
strength and beauty, confident in his magnetic
charm of manner, eager to prove his yet untried
and possibly overestimated abilities, and proudly
anticipating the brilliant future that seemed to
await him. Richelieu, on the other hand, had little
to hope from the future. He had never enjoyed real
health since his boyhood, and he was now a prematurely old man, broken down by sixteen years
of incessant anxiety and uninterrupted labours.
Louis XIII., though a much younger man, was also
in feeble health. During the winter his death had
seemed more than possible, and the conspirators
had busied themselves with schemes for the exclusion of the cardinal from all share in the government during the anticipated minority. The king
had recovered, but he was never more than an in-
valid again, and he was not destined to survive the
cardinal by many months. In spite of their weakness, both king and minister set out early in 1642
to superintend in person the military operations in
Roussillon. Travelling separately and by easy
stages, they both reached Narbonne in March.
There Richelieu, prostrated with fever and tortured by an abscess in his right arm, found that

farther progress was impossible. The doctors advised him to seek a more healthy air in Provence, and Louis XIII., after a delay of more than a month, set out without him to Perpignan (April 21). Richelieu's physical sufferings were thus reinforced by the moral agony which it caused him to part from the king at this critical moment, and thus to leave the field clear for the intrigues of his youthful rival. For another month he remained at Narbonne, detained partly by anxiety and partly by weakness. On May 3, conscious that death was not far distant, he dictated his will to a notary of the town. The bulk of his property he left to his relatives, with the exception of his library, which he bequeathed to the nation, and his residence in Paris, the Palais-Cardinal, which he left to the king, together with the sum of 1,500,-000 livres belonging to the public funds, but which he kept in his own hands for use as occasion might arise. Four days later he set out on his painful journey to Provence.

Richelieu had reached Arles when the long-expected weapon was placed in his hands, in the shape of a copy of the treaty concluded by the conspirators with Spain. How the secret was origi-

nally betrayed has never been known. This proof
of treason he at once despatched to Louis, who
could no longer hesitate to take action. Probably
the danger on this side had never been as great as
the cardinal, in his weakness and mistrust, had
dreaded. Louis had not for a moment dreamed of
seriously balancing the claims of the favourite and
the minister to his confidence. He had listened to
the suggestions and accusations of Cinq-Mars because he had always found it easier to endure than
to check the outbursts of those around him, but on
more than one occasion he had been sufficiently
outspoken to betray his real intention to any one
whose perceptions were not blinded by conceit and
self-confidence. The arrival of Richelieu's communication only hastened a decision that had been already formed. On June 10 he left Perpignan and
returned to Narbonne. Cinq-Mars might still have
escaped by a prompt flight to Sedan, but he recklessly rushed on his fate, and determined to follow
the king. One June 12 the order was issued for the
imprisonment of Cinq-Mars and de Thou, and
messengers were sent to arrest Bouillon in the midst
of the army in Italy, of which he had lately received the command. The king now set out to join

Richelieu at Tarascon, and on June 28 the interview took place in the cardinal's chamber. There
the king and minister, both in bed, agreed upon the
steps to be taken for the maintenance of order and
the punishment of the guilty. Two days later Louis
appointed Richelieu lieutenant-governor of the
kingdom with the full powers of royalty, and set
out on his return to Paris, having neither the
strength nor the inclination to revisit Roussillon.

The collection of evidence against the three
prisoners was not a matter of difficulty. Gaston of
Orleans was ready, as usual, to purchase his own
safety by betraying his associates. He made a full
confession of his relations with Cinq-Mars and of
the treaty with Spain, pleading only that he was
innocent of any plot for the cardinal's assassination. To inflict an adequate punishment on the
king's brother was impossible, but Richelieu seized
the opportunity to humiliate his ancient adversary.
Gaston was compelled to sign a full deposition for
use against his accomplices, and to renounce for the
future all claims to "any office, employment, or
administration in the kingdom." On these terms
he was allowed to reside at Blois as a private individual. Nor did Richelieu spare the king for the

encouragement which, consciously or unconsciously, he had given to the malcontents. Louis XIII. was compelled to turn informer against his quondam favourite, and to confess in a formal document that he had encouraged Cinq-Mars in his freedom of speech and action in order the better to ascertain his real designs, and he asserted that the result of this policy, more worthy of a spy than of a king, was to convince him that his grand equerry was an enemy of the state.

Armed with these depositions, Richelieu set out on August 17 for Lyons by the Rhone, towing his prisoners in another boat behind him. Bouillon had already been sent to Lyons, and there the trial was held before twelve commissioners, including the notorious and indispensable Laubardemont. The guilt of Cinq-Mars was flagrant, and he made no attempt to deny it; but the extent of de Thou's complicity was by no means equally patent. But any hesitation on the part of the judges was removed by the discovery of an ordinance of Louis XI., which declared that the concealment of a plot against the state was an equal offence with actual partnership. The two friends were both condemned to death on September 12, and the sentence was carried out on the same day. Their youth, their rigorous treatment, and the heroism with which they met their fate, have earned for Cinq-Mars and de Thou the sympathy both of contemporaries and posterity. This feeling was intensified by the escape of Bouillon, who was at least equally guilty; but he was the nephew of the prince of Orange, an ally whom France had every reason to conciliate, and he had a valuable hostage for his own life in the fortress of Sedan. On condition that Sedan should be surrendered to the crown, Bouillon obtained a full pardon for his numerous past offences.

The conspiracy of Cinq-Mars was the last episode of importance in the life of Richelieu. The excitement of the struggle had revived for a moment his failing powers, but with its subsidence the process of decline became more rapid than ever. Unable to leave his litter, he was carried slowly from Lyons to Paris, travelling wherever possible by water. Everywhere he was received with the respectful pomp usually displayed only for royalty. In some towns the gates were too narrow to admit the spacious litter, and the wall was promptly demolished to make room for its entry. At Fontainebleau the king came to meet him, and tried to atone for any past coldness by the unusual warmth of his greeting. From Paris Richelieu retired to his favourite residence at Rueil, where he received a visit from the queen, Anne of Austria, who seems to have at last been reconciled with her dying enemy. On November 4 he returned from Rueil to the Palais-Cardinal, which he was never to quit alive.

A sense of exultation may well have buoyed up the spirits of the dying statesman. He was master of France as he had never been before. His domestic enemies were utterly crushed. One of the most inveterate of his opponents, Mary de Medici, had died in this summer at Cologne, endeavouring to the last, by an intentional and exaggerated parade of poverty, to excite odium against the servant of old days whose ingratitude had reduced to such misery and degradation the mother of a French king and of the queens of Spain and England. From all quarters of Europe, from the Pyrenees, from Italy, from Franche Comté, from Germany, the news came of victories which convinced Richelieu that the work of his life was well done, and that the star of the Hapsburgs had paled before that of the Bourbons.

But this feeling of exultation, legitimate as it was, could not quicken his failing pulse, nor expel the fever from his weakened and emaciated frame. On November 29 the mischief spread to his lungs; he began to cough blood, and to experience great difficulty in breathing. Though he lingered for nearly a week, recovery was henceforth impossible. The doctors tried to relieve the fever by frequent bleedings, but the remedy only increased the general weakness. The king paid him two visits, and the cardinal took the opportunity to commend his relatives to the royal protection and favour, and to advise the choice of Mazarin as his own successor. The courage and composure with which he awaited an end which he knew to be inevitable excited the wonder and admiration of all his attendants. His intellect and his iron resolution were alike unaffected by the approach of death. Asked whether he pardoned his enemies, he replied: "Absolutely, and I pray God to condemn me, if I have had any other aim than the welfare of God and of the state."[1] On November 3, the regular physi-

[1]This sentence, like the deathbed utterances of many other eminent men, has been corrupted by tradition into a more epigrammatic form. According to Madame de Motteville, Richelieu replied: "I have had no enemies except those of the state."

cians gave up all hope, and abandoned their patient to an empiric, whose prescriptions produced such a galvanic effect that the rumour of the cardinal's recovery spread through Paris. But the revival was only momentary; in the evening he relapsed into unconsciousness, which was only broken by occasional intervals till the following mid-day, when a groan and a last convulsion of the limbs announced that all was over, and that the man who had been for so many years the great motive-power in France had ceased to live.

Louis XIII.'s studied and habitual coldness of manner enabled him to avoid any display of feeling when the news arrived. "A great politician has departed!" was the only ejaculation that escaped him on hearing of the death of the minister whose greatness so completely overshadowed and obscured his own character. But death did not free him immediately from the influence to which he had so long been accustomed to yield. The wishes of the deceased cardinal were carried out with scrupulous and almost ostentatious fidelity. Mazarin, who for the last year had shared all Richelieu's secrets, was admitted to the council of state the very day after his employer's death, and the other ministers were confirmed in their offices. The lesser posts which were vacated by Richelieu's death were divided among his relatives: the government of Brittany was conferred upon la Meilleraie; the offices of intendant of navigation and governor of Brouage were given to the marquis de Brézé; and the young Armand Jean de Pont-Courlay, who assumed his great-uncle's title of duc de Richelieu, received also the governorship of Havre. A royal circular to the provincial governors and parliaments, dated December 5, announced the king's determination "to maintain all the arrangements made during the ministry of the late cardinal, and to carry out all the plans concerted with him for the conduct of affairs both at home and abroad." A decree for the formal exclusion of the duke of Orleans from the regency, which had been drawn up in deference to Richelieu's wishes, was registered on December 9, in spite of the urgent entreaties of Gaston's daughter, the famous Mademoiselle. The numerous prisoners and exiles, who had hailed the news of the cardinal's death as the signal for their own release and triumph, discovered, to their disgust and disappointment, that no leniency was to be expected from the government.

But no man can continue long to rule from the tomb, and the strenuous and resolute policy of Richelieu was unsuited to the more subtle and agile mind of his successor. Mazarin had all an Italian's love for the refinements of intrigue, and was confident that it was both safer and easier to bend his opponents than to try to break them. Gradually a new policy of leniency and concession was introduced instead of the older methods of stern repression. The prison doors were opened, and the eager exiles were allowed to return to France. The decree against Gaston was revoked, and he was even nominated to the office of lieutenant-governor of the kingdom during the approaching minority. The change of attitude involved dangers and difficulties, which Mazarin may have foreseen, and which he certainly succeeded in the end in overcoming. But Louis XIII., whose growing ill-health made him the passive instrument of his new adviser, did not live to witness the results of the change. His death (May 14, 1643) left his widow and infant son to face the problems of domestic disorder and rebellion, and the consequent prolongation of the war with Spain. That the Fronde proved in the end a harmless and almost a ridiculous movement was due to Richelieu, who had deprived the nobles and parliaments of all substantial power; that the Fronde occurred at all was due to Mazarin's inability to rule with the same iron hand as his more illustrious predecessor.

It is needless to dilate further upon the greatness of Richelieu's achievements, or upon the magnitude of the influence which he exercised upon both France and Europe. That influence was so great and so lasting that it continued to be felt until a new France and a new Europe were evolved from the ruins caused by the Revolution and by the insensate ambition of Napoleon, and even then it was not wholly extinct. In the case of France, indeed, it may be held that the traditions of Richelieu's administration were regarded with excessive and almost fatal veneration. In the next century, when domestic conditions had become almost intolerable, and when wholly new problems had arisen in foreign politics, one generation of ministers after another adhered with blind tenacity and fidelity to the old lines of French policy. By these methods, and under these conditions, France had been raised to greatness, and it was unconsciously argued that to depart from them must result in bringing the country to ruin. Two instances out of many may suffice to illustrate the excessive importance attached to Richelieu's example. In order to check the power of Austria in the east, Richelieu had organised a policy of alliance with three client states—Sweden, Poland, and Turkey. In the eighteenth century these three states had so declined in power that they could no longer serve the purpose for which France had supported them, and in the meantime a wholly new factor had been introduced into eastern politics by the rise of Russia. A great statesman would have seen the necessity of modifying the policy of France to suit these altered conditions, but the French Government persisted in regarding the maintenance of the client states as its primary duty. The result was to alienate Russia and to force her into an unnatural alliance with Austria, and France had in consequence to suffer the profound humiliation of witnessing the partition of Poland without being able to move a finger for its prevention. Again, the dominant aim of Richelieu's foreign policy was to abase the house of Hapsburg, and this end was achieved partly by himself and partly by his successors following in his footsteps. So thoroughly was the work done that in the next century the Hapsburgs had wholly ceased to be formidable to France, and French interests imperatively demanded the maintenance of Austria to secure the balance of power in Europe. But the permanence of the Richelieu tradition prevented France from grasping this patent fact until 1756, and till then the government continued to act as if its primary duty was to erase Austria from the list of great states. This led directly to the elevation of Prussia, destined to deal a terrible blow to French ascendency and prestige, and to the forfeiture to England of the leading part in maritime and colonial enterprise.

It only remains to say something of the character of the great statesman whose career has been sketched in the foregoing pages. It is impossible to contend that Richelieu was wholly admirable as a man, however much admiration may be extorted by his political achievements. His portrait in the Louvre, the masterpiece of Philip of Champagne, impresses the observer with the conviction that he was no vulgar, domineering bully. His clear-cut and delicate features—the white hair contrasting sharply with the dark moustache and

pointed beard—suggest rather the man of letters
or the ascetic priest than the masterful politician
who for so many years dominated both France and
her enemies. But there is the suggestion at once of
power and of irritability in the thin and compressed
lips. One realises that it is the face of a man who
has suffered much, even if he has achieved much; of
a man who has not gained his end without pain
and labour. The fact that Richelieu's health was
never strong, and that he was constantly subject
to physical pain, must be always borne in mind
if we wish really to understand his character and
to appreciate the marvel of the work which he accomplished. From his early manhood he suffered
from excruciating headaches—the result of a fever
contracted in the marshes of Poitou,—and these
often lasted for several days at a time. In one of
his letters he says: "I think I have one of the worst
heads in the world," and adds with a touch of humour not usual with him, "There are many who
will agree with this, but in another sense."

In spite of his physical weakness his industry
was incessant and exhausting. He was not one of
those statesmen who are content to frame the broad
lines of policy and to leave the details to be worked

out by subordinates. Nothing was too small or
unimportant for his attention, though he never lost
sight of the general aim amid the multiplicity of
minute details. His system of spies was the most
extensive and alert that was ever organised by any
statesman. And the activity of his informants was
by no means limited to affairs of state; they had
to bring the latest gossip from the salons, the news
of literary productions and quarrels, the current
talk of the streets and the theatres. The cardinal's
information was always so full and accurate that
it was believed that priests betrayed to him the
secrets of the confessional. On one occasion the
papal nuncio brought him, as a great piece of intelligence, the overtures made by Gaston to the
vice-legate of Avignon. Richelieu acknowledged
the communication by stating the terms of the
answer returned by the vice-legate. But he had to
pay the penalty for his multifarious knowledge in
the enormous amount of labour which it entailed.
Night and day secretaries were in attendance to
copy from his dictation or his rough drafts. Many
of his personal letters were dated in the night. It
was his habit to go to bed about eleven, and after
sleeping for four or five hours to rise and work

till six, when he would return to bed to snatch another brief interval of oblivion till he rose for the day between half-past seven and eight.

The whole weight of affairs rested upon Richelieu. He was not only a first minister, but practically a sole minister. The mistrust inspired by his numerous and watchful enemies impelled him to keep all the strings of home and foreign politics, of military and naval administration, in his own hands; and the responsibility must have been at times almost overwhelming to a man who lived a life so essentially solitary. Nothing in Richelieu's career is more striking than his isolation. He had dependents, flatterers, and tools in plenty; but with the exception of the mysterious Father Joseph he had no confidential friend, no one with whom he could freely discuss personal and public affairs, no one who could relieve him of some part of his burden by sharing his secrets and anxieties. He was extremely inaccessible; even foreign envoys could only gain admission to his presence when the business to be discussed was of special importance. He never quitted his residence without the attendance of his personal bodyguard, paid from his own purse and officered by his own nominees. Even in the

royal palace he insisted upon retaining their services. It was this habit of jealous suspicion, rather
than the prompting of family affection, that led
him to promote to high office his own relatives, as
his brother-in-law, de Brézé, his cousin, la Meilleraie, and his nephew, de Pont-Courlay. His own
colleagues in the ministry were little more than
clerks who carried out instructions received from
the cardinal.

The burden of labour and responsibility which
devolved upon Richelieu, partly by his own choice
and partly by compulsion, must have been rendered
all the heavier by the extraordinary uncertainty of
his own position. The king's health was never
strong, and on several occasions his life was in
serious danger from disease. If he had died at any
time before the birth of the dauphin—born, it
must be remembered, after twenty-two years of
barren wedlock—the royal power, which Richelieu
himself had so immensely strengthened, would have
passed at once to the cardinal's arch-enemy, Gaston
of Orleans. Nor was Richelieu's hold over Louis
XIII. by any means secure, at any rate in the earlier
years of his ministry. Louis was no mere puppet, as
has been often represented. His understanding was

retentive though slow; he took a keen interest in
public business, especially in its details, and he had
a large share of the obstinacy and self-confidence
of his mother. In order to obtain and keep the
king's confidence, in spite of the domestic and
other influences always at work against him, Richelieu had to act with great tact and caution. He
never ventured to take any step without the
king's consent, and it is certain that Louis would
never have tolerated such an assertion of independent authority. Hence the necessity of constant
conferences or correspondence, which the courtiers
hoped and believed would so bore the king that he
would ultimately seek to escape from such enthrall-
ing conditions. On every minute point of policy
and administration Richelieu found it necessary not
only to convince Louis—in itself a toilsome task—
but also to create in his mind the impression that
the ultimate decision was not the overmastering
will of the minister but the independent product
of the royal intellect. While Richelieu was so stern
and awe-inspiring towards the outside world, he
had to play the supple and pliant courtier in the
presence of the master on whose favour and confidence all his own authority was based.

The charge most frequently brought against Richelieu is that of cruelty and vindictiveness, and it is a charge that cannot possibly be denied. Among the victims who perished on the scaffold for opposition to his rule were "five dukes, four counts, a marshal of France, and the king's favourite equerry, Cinq-Mars." To these must be added a number of lesser offenders who were put to death, and the many opponents, of all ranks, who were condemned to imprisonment in the Bastille or driven into exile in foreign lands by the minister whose enmity they had incurred. But if Richelieu was pitiless, he was not, like most revengeful despots, either capricious or unjust. He did not strike the tool if he could reach the employer; nor did he strike till guilt was obvious and incontestable; his was no reckless reign of terror. His methods, though often arbitrary and contrary to legal custom and tradition, were always fearless and above-board. Political considerations sometimes made it impossible to inflict a fitting penalty upon men who richly deserved it, such as de Bouillon and the traitorous Gaston, but the motive that allowed them to escape was never terror nor a wish to curry favour. And the experience of Mazarin's administration supplies a retrospective

justification for Richelieu's severity. He was undoubtedly right from his own point of view in
acting upon the maxim of Machiavelli that "it is
safer to be feared than to be loved." It was the
sense of impunity that had made the nobles independent and rebellious; this feeling had been
strengthened by the concessions and pardons of the
regency, and the only way to remove it and to compel obedience was by making their punishments
prompt, severe, and impartial. The element of personal resentment, which seems to disfigure and condemn Richelieu's pitiless treatment of his foes, is
accounted for by the sublime confidence with
which he identified his own ascendency with the
welfare of the state, a confidence without which
few rulers have been able to achieve really great
work. Finally, whatever we may think of the
morality of Richelieu's actions, it is impossible not
to be impressed by the magnificent courage with
which, almost single-handed, he faced the most
powerful nobles of the land, allied as they were
with members of the royal family, and backed
up from outside by great foreign powers. And
this courage becomes the more memorable when we
remember that Richelieu was no demagogue, sup-

ported by the enthusiastic and encouraging applause of the masses of the people. On the contrary,
the successes which attended France were obscured
to contemporaries by the material sufferings which
were caused by military expenditure and defective financial wisdom. In his later years Richelieu was detested by the populace, and it is said
that bonfires were kindled in many provinces of
the kingdom to celebrate the death of the statesman who has been hailed by the almost unanimous
opinion of later generations as the grandest figure
among those who have contributed most to the
greatness of France.

APPENDIX A

GENEALOGY OF THE RICHELIEU FAMILY

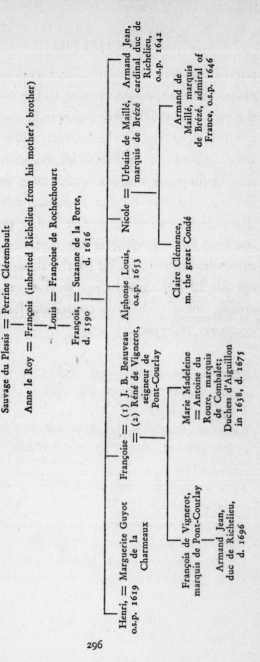

Sauvage du Plessis = Perrine Clérembault

Anne le Roy = François (inherited Richelieu from his mother's brother)

Louis = Françoise de Rochechouart

François, = Suzanne de la Porte,
d. 1590   d. 1616

Henri, = Marguerite Guyot de la Charmeaux
o.s.p. 1619

Françoise = (1) J. B. Beauveau
= (2) Réné de Vignerot, seigneur de Pont-Courlay

Alphonse Louis, o.s.p. 1653

Nicole = Urbain de Maillé, marquis de Brézé

Armand Jean, cardinal duc de Richelieu, o.s.p. 1642

Marie Madeleine = Antoine du Roure, marquis de Combalet; Duchess d'Aiguillon in 1638, d. 1675

François de Vignerot, marquis de Pont-Courlay

Armand Jean, duc de Richelieu, d. 1696

Claire Clémence, m. the great Condé

Armand de Maillé, marquis de Brézé, admiral of France, o.s.p. 1646

APPENDIX B

THE CHIEF BOOKS ON THE PERIOD

I HAVE not attempted to compile a complete bibliography of writings on the age of Richelieu, nor even to draw up a list of all the authorities which I have consulted. My only object is to call the attention of the reader, who may wish to make a more detailed study of the period, to those books which he is likely to find most helpful and accessible.

Richelieu, *Mémoires*, 1610–1638 (Petitot's collection, 2nd series, xxi.-xxx.; Michaud et Poujoulat, 2nd series, vii.-ix.).

Richelieu, *Succincte narration des grandes actions du Roi* (Petitot, 2nd series, xi.; Michaud et Poujoulat, 2nd series, ix.).

Richelieu, *Lettres, Instructions Diplomatiques et Papiers d'État*, edited by M. d'Avenel. Paris, 8 volumes, 1853–1877.

Harangue pour la présentation des cahiers, ou clôture de l'assemblée, aux États, prononcé par l'évêque de Luçon, orateur du clergé (Petitot, 2nd series, xi., p. 201).

Fontenay-Mareuil, *Mémoires* (Petitot, 1st series, l., li; Michaud et Poujoulat, 2nd series, v.).

Bassompierre, *Mémoires* (Michaud et Poujoulat, 2nd series, vi.).

De Brienne, *Mémoires* (Michaud et Poujoulat, 3rd series, iii.; Petitot, 2nd series, xxxv., xxxvi.).

D'Estrées, *Mémoires* (Michaud et Poujoulat, 2nd series, vi.).

De Pontis, *Mémoires* (Michaud et Poujoulat, 2nd series, vi.).

Mathieu Molé, *Mémoires* (Société de l'Histoire de France, Paris, 1855–1857).

Omer-Talon, *Mémoires* (Michaud et Poujoulat, 3rd series, vi.).

Arnauld d'Andilly, *Mémoires* (Michaud et Poujoulat, 2nd series, ix.).

Madame de Motteville, *Mémoires* (Michaud et Poujoulat, 2nd series, x.).

De Rohan, *Mémoires* (1610–1629) and *Mémoires sur la Guerre de la Valtelline* (Michaud et Poujoulat, 2nd series, v.).

Montchal, *Mémoires* (Rotterdam, 1718).

Aubéry, *L'Histoire du Cardinal-Duc de Richelieu* (Paris, 1660; Cologne, 2 volumes, 1666).

Aubéry, *Mémoires pour l'histoire du Cardinal-Duc de Richelieu* (Paris, 1660; Cologne, 5 volumes, 1667).

Martineau, *Le Cardinal de Richelieu*, tome i. (Paris, 1870).

Hanotaux, *Histoire du Cardinal de Richelieu*, tome i., *La jeunesse de Richelieu*, 1585–1614 (Paris, 1893).

Griffet, *Histoire du Règne de Louis XIII.* (Paris, 1758).

Bazin, *Histoire de France sous Louis XIII. et sous le ministère du Cardinal Mazarin* (4 volumes, Paris, 1846, 2nd edition).

Henri Martin, *Histoire de France*, tome xi. (4th edition, Paris, 1859).

Ranke, *Französische Geschichte, vornehmlich im sechszehnten und siebzehnten Jahrhundert*, Band ii. (Leipzig, 1876, Vierte Auflage).

D'Avenel, *Richelieu et la Monarchie Absolue* (4 volumes, Paris, 1884–1892).

Topin, *Louis XIII. et Richelieu, Étude Historique, accompagnée des lettres inédites du Roi au Cardinal de Richelieu* (2nd edition, Paris, 1876).

Caillet, *L'Administration en France sous le ministère du Cardinal de Richelieu* (Paris, 1857).

APPENDIX C

THE *TESTAMENT POLITIQUE*

ONE of the most keenly-debated points in connection with Richelieu is that of the authenticity of the *Testament Politique*, which was originally published at Amsterdam in 1688, and of which I have consulted the Paris edition of 1764. The first chapter, which has been printed in the collections of M. Petitot and of MM. Michaud and Poujoulat, under the title of *Succincte narration des grandes actions du Roi*, has been generally admitted to be a genuine work of the cardinal's, and to be equally authentic with the *Memoirs*. With this view I entirely agree. But the second chapter, the *Testament* proper, to which the *Succincte narration* serves as a sort of introduction, has been the subject of much discussion from the time of Voltaire downwards. In the present century there has been a growing tendency to treat it as an authoritative statement of Richelieu's political opinions in his later years. M. Henri Martin goes so far as to say that "the genius of the cardinal, whatever may be said to the contrary, is as obvious in the complete *Testament* as in the first chapter: the lion's mark is to be traced in a thousand passages, and the powerful personality of Richelieu is revealed by a crowd of traits which the abbé de Bourzeis could never have invented." This very positive opinion seems to me to be wholly untenable. The external evidence is quite indecisive one way or the other, but the internal evidence, both of style and matter, seems to be conclusive against the authenticity of the work. It is possible that the general plan may have been sketched out by Richelieu and filled in by a subordinate, but in that case it can hardly have undergone the cardinal's revision, and its value as evidence of his opinions is almost as slight as if it were an intentional forgery; and the latter seems to me to be, on the whole, much the more probable solution. In accordance with this conviction I have carefully abstained— in spite of obvious temptations to the contrary—from making any use of the *Testament* as a guide to the real aims of Richelieu's policy. And I am further of opinion that, if its authenticity could be conclusively proved, the current estimates of Richelieu would have to be not merely added to, but profoundly modified. Especially the striking saying of Mignet, that "he intended everything which he achieved," would have to be abandoned, and many results of his rule, which are now attributed to intelligent purpose, would have to be regarded as the product of chance.

THE END